P9-DNR-587

RUSSIA'S

CHILDREN

A First Report on Child Welfare in the Soviet Union

RUSSIA'S CHILDREN

By Herschel and Edith Alt

Bookman Associates, New York

manufactured in the United States of America

DESIGNED BY SIDNEY SOLOMON

PRINTED FOR THE PUBLISHERS
BY UNITED PRINTING SERVICES, INC., NEW HAVEN

LIBRARY OF CONGRESS CATALOG CARD NUMBER: 59-8398

TO ALL CHILDREN EVERYWHERE

THAT THEY MAY GROW UP

WITH LOVE, WITH FREEDOM AND WITH TRUTH

Acknowledgments

A LIST of everyone who helped to make our visit rewarding would be so long as to exceed the practical possibilities of enumeration. We feel especially grateful to the staffs of the American Embassy in Moscow and the Soviet Embassy in Washington for their many courtesies and helpful suggestions.

We particularly wish to express our thanks to Leo Gruliow, editor of *The Current Digest of the Soviet Press,* who shared with us his rich knowledge of Russian life before we went to the Soviet Union and after our return; to Elena Calas, for verification of the facts on child-rearing practices in the Soviet Union and some of the inferences we drew from our observations; to Helen Buckler and Ruth L. Tolins, for editorial assistance in the preparation of the manuscript.

THE AUTHORS

Contents

PART ONE

The Struggle to See and Learn

I

Why We Went to Soviet Russia

AT LEAST two thousand Americans from all walks of life visited the Soviet Union during the summer of 1956 and an equal number in 1957. Each had his special reason for wanting to see what was taking place there. This was true for my wife and myself.

We are social workers. In different ways we have invested our energies for many years in promoting better opportunities for a fuller life for people in our own country. Each has specialized in a phase of social work, but we have also achieved a common point of view about the rights of the individual and how these can be reconciled with the well-being of the group.

Edith Alt's special interest is in health services and medical care; more particularly, in the social and psychological problems of individuals and families beset by illness.

For many years I have been interested in the care of the socially disadvantaged child—the homeless, the neglected, the delinquent, the emotionally disturbed.

Both of us are concerned in our daily work with the treatment of psychological problems, with psychiatric care, and with community plans to provide these services whether through voluntary or governmental programs. Both of us have had considerable technical experience in the work of assessing community needs and resources in these fields.

Previous official visits to Israel, Venezuela, Germany, Yugoslavia had given me, I felt, a broader and sharper perspective on our own American aspirations and methods, a keener awareness of both differences and similarities in what nations want for their children, and a clearer realization of the interplay between social organization and purpose, on the one hand, and the principles and methods of child rearing on the other.

We were eager to see in what ways the Soviet Union's approach to the task of child rearing differed from our own. This interest gained in importance when we realized that the international bodies, including the United Nations, had very little information and almost no reports from observers on child care in the Soviet Union. A preliminary review of available data based on eyewitness accounts found such amazingly meager material that it might be called practically nonexistent. Whatever we could bring back would be valuable.

But such a visit promised other possible gains. Only as we add to our understanding of the interrelatedness of social phenomena and social process can we hope to participate effectively in the guidance of social change. In this context, the Soviet enterprise represents a social laboratory of the first importance, embodying as it does the most radical contemporary effort in any part of the world to condition human beings to meet social demands.

Unlike other nations and societies in which revolutionary changes are taking place, the Soviet Union is attempting an almost complete reconstruction of a total social order. It has outlined clearly defined political, economic and social forms embracing not only basic changes in institutions but also clearly articulated standards for approved human behavior. The Soviet Union has also defined its image of the ideal citizen. How it is going about to mold the human personality from babyhood, with what success or failure, is a matter of deep interest to every student of child rearing and human relations.

It is well known to those professionally engaged in comprehending broad social scenes that it is sometimes easier for the outsider than the native to grasp the interrelationship of forces at work. No apology therefore is needed for the outsider who attempts to understand a situation foreign to his own. At the same time, the outsider is bound to admit his data are necessarily incomplete and his conclusions tentative. This is true of this report.

Our observations in other foreign countries have yielded a broader perspective on our own problems. Sometimes the experiences have highlighted a particular aspect of our work; sometimes yielded new clues and new starting points for profitable efforts in helping children in our own country. Sometimes these observations have provided warnings and danger signals.

It is difficult to sort out our personal reasons for going to Russia from those which are more professional. A lifetime of professional experience becomes part of a person—of his feelings, attitudes and values. It is the frame of reference he brings to every new possibility and situation.

Nonetheless, we did have personal reasons. I* was born and spent my first seven years in Byelorussia. A Jewish child's memories of life in Russia in the early 1900's must necessarily remain a mixture of apprehensiveness and childhood pleasures: fear that the *pogromchiks* would come and destroy us and at the same time warm assurance that, if they did, the Russian family sharing our yard would hang their ikons on our walls and hide my brother and me in their home. I recall the violence of the army recruits during the week of their induction and how during that week we closed up our yard and barred our house shutters early every evening. I also recall the little Russian girl who was my favorite playmate and the friendly town advocate who fed me candies and advised my mother in her business affairs until she could take us and follow my father, after a delay of five years, to Canada.

Time has tempered the hurts and mellowed the pleasures with nostalgia so that emotional ties to Russia and these friendly people remain. Canada, where I spent my youth and

* Except in Chapter XII, the first person pronoun refers to Herschel Alt. In Chapter XII it refers to Edith Alt.

received my formal education, claims much personal interest, too. And so does Israel which represents a future for displaced Jews and an essential ingredient in the self-respect of Jews everywhere. The United States, my home, where I have spent most of my adult life and to the welfare of whose children I have given my thought and energy for more than thirty years, is the center of my interest, the crowning consideration in my ventures toward understanding other nations.

Though born in Connecticut, my wife is the daughter of Russian immigrants who came to the United States in their early years. Their tales of Russia, told over and over again in her childhood, left such a deep imprint that she felt she even knew the stickiness of the muddy roads they described.

Our interest in what happens to the children of Russia goes beyond personal and professional interests. As members of families faced with establishing themselves in new surroundings among strangers and strange ways, we were early sensitized to social issues and problems in human relationships. We both have dreamed of a better world. What a country wants for its children and the way it goes about achieving it, we feel, is the best indicator of the level of its social evolution.

II

We Prepare for the Trip

WITH THE LIFTING of travel restrictions to the Soviet Union, I immediately resumed efforts begun ten years earlier to arrange for an observational visit to that land. Our preparations began in the autumn of 1955.

We talked with the New York representative of Intourist, the official Soviet travel agency. We went to Washington to get some idea of the interest of certain of the key staff members of the United States Department of Health, Education, and Welfare in the child welfare situation in the Soviet Union. We talked with representatives of the United States State Department and with the staff at the Soviet Embassy. We also made a point of talking with recent visitors to the Soviet Union to learn whether they might have helpful suggestions for planning the trip and particularly how we might assure ourselves that we would have access to those phases of child life in the Soviet Union within our particular fields of interest.

In January we began correspondence with VOKS, the Soviet agency for cultural relations. We explained as clearly as we could the purpose of our visit, describing the nature of our work in this country and our spheres of interest—medical care and educational programs for children with special reference to child rearing and child guidance and the care and treatment of the delinquent and mentally ill child.

After a number of letters VOKS told us that while it would

not be possible to extend an "official invitation," everything would be done to enable us to meet our "opposite numbers." In addition, we wrote to a number of key professional workers in the health, educational and child care fields in the Soviet Union. To each, we outlined our interest in observing the fields of child rearing and education, and specifically the treatment of emotionally disturbed, neglected and delinquent children. With few exceptions, we received replies from all the professional workers to whom we wrote. These included the director of a psychological hospital for children, a central psychiatric dispensary, the Ministry of Public Health and the Academy of Pedagogical Sciences, the Pavlovian Institute of Physiology, and many others. Some of the officials informed us that they might be out of the city on vacation during the period of our visit but they would have someone else in their establishment meet us.

At the same time I began relearning the Russian language and achieved sufficient competence so that I was able to read signs, have some understanding of printed material, read menus and carry on a simple conversation.

Both of us also read a number of books that we felt might provide a background of understanding. *The Current Digest of the Soviet Press* proved particularly helpful. Thus, before we went to Russia we knew from our reading about such diverse matters as the structure of the Ministry of Health, the medical care program, the new ten-year educational program, the way youthful crime and delinquency are written about in the Russian newspapers. We had read articles scolding parents for pampering their children and others scolding bureaucrats for malfeasance in office.

We did not, like some tourists we later saw in Russia, arm ourselves with photographs and other evidence of the high economic standards of American life. We were not going to propagandize, or, if we could help it, to be propagandized. Our interests were professional, not political. We wanted to meet people on natural, friendly terms, not to stir up feelings by thoughtless or irritating questions. Our hope was to keep everything as much as possible on an objective, factual level.

III

We Set Foot on Russian Soil

THE FIRST IMPRESSIONS a visitor receives in a new country are important. They create a certain mindset for experiences which follow.

What impressed us most in our first hours on Russian soil and remained with us throughout the visit was a strong sense of contrast and contradiction. True, all nations and civilizations are characterized in varying degrees by inconsistency and disharmony in various aspects of their life. It would not be surprising that the Soviet Union, an extensive country covering a large part of the globe and including many ethnic groups with sharply different historical experience, should present many differences, if it were not for the professed clarity of goals and the emphasis on unity and equality. Whether the sharp contrasts represent a lag between purpose and implementation, or more basic questions about the purposes themselves, these contrasts present a good starting point for further study of the social and psychological milieux in Soviet Russia.

We left Copenhagen during the mid-afternoon, en route to Leningrad. Our tickets had been purchased in New York with specific dates for arrival and departure at Copenhagen, Leningrad, Moscow and Kiev.

The plane which we were to board at Copenhagen was to go on to Moscow. It would take us as far as Riga where we planned to change to a plane for Leningrad.

With two friends who traveled with us,* we were eager and curious for our first glimpse of a Russian plane. But the time of departure from Copenhagen arrived and our plane was nowhere to be seen. Finally, the departure was announced and we were led to the extreme end of the field, perhaps as far away as two city blocks. "Did the Russians avoid contacts with foreigners, or what?," we wondered.

The *Aeroflot* turned out to be a two-engine plane that might be described as a cross between a DC-3 and a Convair. It was different from any plane we had used in Europe: two dozen seats, none with seat belts, and comfortable though plain upholstery. None of the planes we traveled on in Russia had seat belts and we found we could manage quite well without them. Our trip was uneventful. About fifteen people were aboard—a group of five or six Canadian lumbermen, about the same number of Russians, a Scandinavian Airlines System representative, and ourselves. A buffet held apples, soda water and a steaming tea samovar. A table held Russian magazines.

After a three-hour trip we arrived in Riga and disembarked in the dusk. A cold drizzle was falling. We had come only 4000 miles from torrid New York, but we had skipped the calendar from July to November. It was comforting to leave the dismal outdoors for the brightly lighted airport. This building was spacious and clean, certainly adequate, if not elegant.

Here we had our first encounter with Russian immigration, customs and Intourist personnel. There was no lack of courtesy in the routines of passport clearance, currency declaration and customs check, all of which were handled without inconvenience. One was struck, however, with the overabundance of personnel. Each official had two or three assistants and there was confusion about regulations among them. Passports were taken away, returned, and then taken away again a number of times.

Among the many attendants a young woman, about thirty

---

* We were accompanied on our trip by Mrs. Henry Ittleson, Sr., and her grandson, Henry Ittleson III.

years old, stood out for her brisk, efficient manner. She spoke excellent English. Edith thought she was a little too efficient, too sharp and "bossy." She dubbed her "the Sergeant" because of her briskness.

We had plenty of time before our plane was scheduled to depart and were told to go upstairs for dinner. We found ourselves in a large, plain room, half-filled with perhaps seventy-five diners. Waiters in white jackets and waitresses in large white aprons went about their duties slow-moving, almost lackadaisical in manner. A four-piece orchestra of middle-aged men, corpulent, colorless, played mechanically. I was reminded of orchestras I had heard in Yugoslavia two years earlier playing with no spontaneity whatever and leaving the listener disturbed rather than pleased. This Riga orchestra certainly added no gaiety to the drab scene.

We would have ended our dinner happily had not the official we called the "Sergeant" suddenly appeared at my elbow and announced without introduction or apology:

"You will stay here for forty-eight hours. Then you will go to Leningrad."

"But why?"

"There is no place for your party on the plane to Leningrad," she said.

"What do you mean?" I exclaimed. "We have our reservations and they were confirmed."

The "Sergeant" simply reiterated "There is no place" and when I suggested telephoning the head office in Moscow, she answered, "No long distance calls are allowed." I suggested wiring and received the answer, "No telegrams allowed."

I turned to the Scandinavian Airlines representative who was seated at a nearby table and explained the situation to him. There was little he could do except to assure us that we were right and a mistake had occurred. He intimated that this frequently happened.

We could not face the prospect of spending two days of our short visit in the Riga airport. When we discovered there was still space on the plane which had brought us from Copenhagen and was now proceeding to Moscow, we decided to go on to Moscow instead of Leningrad although this entailed some risk of discomfort since our hotel reservations in Moscow were for five days hence. We felt, however, that whatever the discomfort might be, we would have to face it.

I told the ticket agent we would go on to Moscow. He tore out two of our coupons: Riga-to-Leningrad and Leningrad-to-Moscow.

"What do we use to get to Leningrad from Moscow?" I asked. He shrugged his shoulders. I asked for a receipt. He refused. I asked again. In excellent English he said, "I am not putting my name to any piece of paper."

At this point I became cautious too. I went personally to see that our luggage got aboard this plane. I found three porters, sallow, middle-aged men in grey denim pants and over-blouses. They moved flabbily, picked up the bags slowly, spoke in whispers. They seemed to have no muscle tone, scarcely to be alive. To a man standing nearby who was obviously Jewish, I put the question traveling Jews ask each other the world over.

"How goes it with Jews here?"

"Hard," he whispered, "very hard."

The plane was announced and we hurried out. Sidling along the outer wall of the building I saw a shabbily dressed young woman. Her clumsy thick black skirt was torn and partially patched; her jacket was out at the elbows. With her were two children, a girl and a boy, six and eight perhaps. They wore clothes several sizes too big and very shabby. The faces of all three were pasty white.

We were relieved to get back in the familiar plane. It was bright and dry. The samovar steamed cozily. Edith picked up one of the Russian magazines and I followed suit. It was a *de luxe* publication, more "slick" than our *Life* magazine. Flipping the pages I saw handsome photographs—a new model hospital—new equipment for processing coal. And then my startled eye fell on an article exhorting the Soviet citizen to put money in the savings bank every month and pointing out all the advantages of savings. I would have recognized these arguments as appropriate back home but weren't they totally unnecessary in a communist state?

Taking the magazine I wandered back and sat down with the hostess, a pleasant homespun girl, large and rawboned, wearing a simple uniform. She had none of the svelte delicacy considered good public relations by American companies, but she was a friendly capable girl. She spoke a little French and this with my limited Russian and the photographs in the magazine enabled us to carry on a conversation of sorts. By the time we reached Moscow I had learned a few new Russian words and was again in an eager mood.

With our arrival in Moscow at one A.M. the rain stopped and our luck seemed to have turned. The airport was relatively small for a city of the importance of Moscow. In size it was like the one at Rochester, New York, or Minneapolis, but more impressive. Marble pillars and a bust of Lenin enhanced the entrance to a new reception building with upstairs restaurant. The Intourist waiting room was pleasant and well furnished.

I told the Intourist agent our story. We had no hotel reservations for this date. Could we get into a hotel? Within a half-hour he had a reservation for us and put us into a ZIS car for our trip to the city. Of the four types of cars made in the Soviet Union the hand-assembled luxury ZIS is tops. It is the car of officialdom, so we felt very well treated.

Edith pointed to the dark window curtains behind which we, like top officials on a secret mission, might hide. We pushed them back and craned our necks. At first, in the dim early light, we could see only open fields interspersed with dark patches of forest. As our eyes grew accustomed to the dimness, we saw the roads were not entirely deserted even at this hour. We passed several men with fishing poles over their shoulders, striding along purposefully. After forty minutes the lights of Moscow appeared. With what Russian I could command, I pressed the chauffeur with questions. He obliged by pointing out various floodlighted towers—the imposing, modern, twenty-story Moscow University, the seven bizarre, onion-topped towers of ancient St. Basil's Church, the crenellated walls of the venerable Kremlin.

We were delighted to find ourselves assigned to the National Hotel on the corner of Mokhovaya Street and Gorki Boulevard, only half a block from the Red Square. We got out of our car around two A.M. The streets were filled, despite the hour, with pedestrians. They were as crowded as Times Square at the theater hour. But these people were not loitering and laughing, they were hurrying by, silently, most of them carrying bundles. Without stopping to wonder where they were going at such an hour, we hastened in to find ourselves in the most interesting of Moscow's four hotels for foreign visitors.

The National, with two floors of lounges, dining rooms and offices and three floors of perhaps fifty or sixty bedrooms, was impressive with its old-world character. It has spacious lobbies and halls, beautiful staircases, paneled walls, luxurious hangings, crystal chandeliers and the fine furniture and oriental rugs of the old regime. Edith was given a room large enough to hold a reception in—more of a drawing-room than a bedroom, with two large sofas, several wardrobes, and lovely Chinese lacquer furniture, museum pieces, decorated in gold and rich crimson and inlaid with mother-of-pearl. Her bed, however, was a narrow, though comfortable, couch tucked away in a curtained alcove. Spacious though the room was, sleeping arrangements could not be stretched to two persons.

Apologizing because they could not give me a similar room until next day, the night clerk led me to smaller quarters where I slept very well, grateful for a big feather-filled comforter.

The next day started auspiciously and none of the dire reports we had heard about Soviet living conditions proved true. The plumbing was old-fashioned, but it worked and there was plenty of hot water. I dressed in a winter suit and went to Edith's room for breakfast. She was dressed in her warmest clothing, too. These, incidentally, we were to wear almost our entire trip, although it was in July and August.

There was no fruit, but we breakfasted happily on fresh rolls, farm eggs and delicious hot tea, waited on by an excellent servant, a gnarled old man who seemed, like the hotel itself, a relic from former times. Rudolf bowed and scraped and was ready to accept a tip. Here was another of our constant surprises. We had been warned not to insult the Soviet citizen with tips. This old fellow, like many others, would have been disappointed indeed had we followed such advice, and we did not. Tipping, we found, was all right if you did it privately.

IV

Our Struggle with Intourist

THE QUESTION we were most frequently asked on our return to America was: "Did you see what you wanted to see?"

The answer was: "Only in part." But when we began to amplify this answer, the listener was usually impressed with the fact that we were allowed to see as much as we did. During our visit, however, we were constantly involved in a struggle with the Intourist personnel to arrange for us to talk to certain persons or visit certain establishments. These were not the designated places on the official Intourist list which is made available to tourists before they leave the United States, such as the museums, collective farms, parks and theaters. Children's nurseries and kindergartens are often included as well.

Our struggle to gain access to certain kinds of information, to observe certain institutions, continued in one form or another throughout our visit. Despite our correspondence with VOKS and direct communication with certain ministries and leading workers, we were not able to break through to our first professional visit without a great deal of struggle with the Intourist personnel. We finally had to take the position that we would make visits independently if Intourist did not complete the arrangements. Only then was the necessary telephoning undertaken and the appointments made.

It is significant that doors which were originally closed to us were opened after a good deal of pleading and pressure on our part. This was true of conferences with the Ministry of Social Security, the Council of Trade Unions, the Ministry of Internal Affairs and even of a visit to a People's Court and a home for the aged.

While many visitors who had a special interest in learning about some particular phase of Russian life told us of difficulties in getting to see what they wanted, it is hard to say how far their experience corresponded to our own. It may be that professional visitors interested in the theater, or in the musical field, or some particular industry or less sensitive areas of Russian life, have had less difficulty.

No doubt our struggle and frustration in getting to see certain things influenced our feelings about the total experience. Whether difficulties we encountered were due to official policy, to the inability of the Intourist personnel to exercise judgment and discretion within the rules set for them, is hard for us to say. However, if the difficulty of getting to see things is viewed objectively, it throws light on many aspects of Russian life and on the forces which shape human behavior and the mold of the individual.

We undertook the trip with a clear purpose which involved considerable personal and financial expense and were, therefore, eager to make every minute count. Immediately after breakfast on the first Tuesday morning in Moscow, we went to the Intourist office, taking the folder which included letters from VOKS, the Soviet Embassy in Washington, as well as others in the Soviet Union with whom we corresponded. This office was found on the second floor in our own hotel, not more than fifty yards from our rooms. We were to spend many hours here in the Intourist office, so it may be worth describing.

Entering frosted glass doors, we found ourselves in a medium-sized room crowded with many desks, personnel and perhaps eight or ten tourists, every one trying to get cars or guides or theater tickets. Opposite the door was a table with magazines and several wicker chairs for the tourists. At the right was a desk where sat a man who appeared to be the boss.

Ranging down the room with an aisle between were a half-dozen desks, a girl clerk at each. Each girl dealt, we learned, with a particular matter: theater tickets, passports, transportation, cars, chauffeurs, and so on. Each had several notebooks in which she recorded the tourists' requests. There were no typewriters. On the walls were some maps and a theater list. Several tourists were gathered around a mimeographed digest of news in English.

Somewhat uncertainly I approached the chief. It was impossible to speak with him privately. People crowded around his desk and everyone heard everyone else's business. I waited my turn and studied the man. He was heavy-set, perhaps forty, partly bald with a smooth face, brisk agreeable manner. At the moment he was on the telephone being very hale and hearty in excellent English. Later we learned his name was Ivanov, that he was an ex-newspaperman, and that he loved to spend Sundays searching the nearby woods for mushrooms.

Ivanov finished talking and acknowledged my presence. I presented our requests as clearly as possible. I went over the correspondence and handed him a list of persons with whom we would like to have appointments. I also gave him an envelope addressed to Mme. Katerina Furtseva, the only woman member of the Central Presidium of the Communist party and reputed to be the highest official interested in the problems of families and children. This envelope included a copy of a letter I had sent her while still in the United States to which I had not received a reply before leaving for Russia. I asked him if he would see that the letter got to her.

"I will mail it," said Ivanov, "but do not expect an answer."

I asked why not and he said, "Well, you understand your letter, like everyone else's, will start at the bottom and pass through maybe a dozen hands before it gets to Mme. Furtseva, and whether it gets to her, we won't know."

"But *someone* will surely acknowledge it," I said. He shrugged and disappeared behind the dark velvet curtain which separated the waiting room from inner offices where, we later learned, the guides and the central Intourist staff carried on their business and which was not open to the public. Shortly he returned with a fair-skinned, blue-eyed blonde girl twenty or twenty-one years old.

"This is Miss Katrina Nikolaevska," he said. "She is our best guide-interpreter. She will take care of you."

We smiled and bowed. Ivanov moved away. We were interested in the slim, graceful girl in whose hands the success of our visit might lie—our *alter ego* who would make our appointments, take us where we wanted to go, ask our questions for us, and give us the answers.

Fortunately Katrina spoke excellent English fluently. Her manner was cheerful. We were touched by her efforts to make herself look smart despite a colorless suit, unadorned nylon blouse and clumsy shoes. Given attractive clothes, Katrina would have been a beautiful girl.

I handed Katrina the list of professional appointments we wished to make. She did not look at it.

"Of course, first," she said, "you will want to see the Kremlin and the Mausoleum and to go out to the Agricultural Exhibition."

"Not yet," I said, "our time is very limited. After we have visited ministries, clinics, children's nurseries and the home for delinquent boys, then we will go sightseeing. Besides, everything we see on the way to these places will be sightseeing for us. Everything here is new and interesting to us."

Glancing at my watch and seeing it was already half-past ten, I opened the folder of correspondence. "Let's start here," I said, "with the Pedagogical Institute. Please call and say we are here and would like an appointment to see the director. Here is his letter. You see it is very cordial. Or, if you can't get him for today, try VOKS. They know all about our interests."

With unsmiling face Katrina disappeared behind the velvet curtain. We waited. After a half-hour she returned.

"Where do we go first?" I asked.

Katrina smiled deprecatingly. "These things take time," she said, "Perhaps tomorrow you will have an appointment. Now we can go sightseeing."

I tried to pin Katrina down to what people had said. If not today, then when could we see these people? All I could get from her were vague statements of "not in." But when would he be in, I asked, and if not this one, then the other one. Her answer was the same: Not in, and apparently no one knew when anyone would be in. In the end we went sightseeing. Somehow I felt this was Katrina's plan all along.

As we went out of the hotel to get in our car, Edith said, "Let's stop at the American Embassy first. We want to pick up our mail."

To our complete mystification, our pretty guide's delicate face flushed an angry red. Her answer came quick, sharp-edged, "I do not wish to go with you to the American Embassy. You can go alone. The chauffeur will take you. I will see you later."

At the Embassy we registered, picked up our mail and had a short talk with Ambassador Charles E. Bohlen who was interested in our project and made many helpful suggestions to us. He concluded our talk by remarking: "But, frankly, Alt, I doubt very much that you will get to see any home for delinquent boys."

"They exist, don't they?" I asked.

"Oh yes, undoubtedly they exist," he answered, "but seeing them is another matter."

As we finished our lunch at the hotel, Katrina sent word she was waiting with the car. Her good humor was restored, perhaps because she was to show us the magnificence of her country.

Bright and early Wednesday morning at the Intourist office the real struggle for appointments began. Again Katrina was designated as our guide and again we were at the mercy of her stubborn defensiveness. No appointments had been made and she was again bent on having us follow the scheduled sightseeing tour.

I turned to Ivanov. Of course, in those crowded quarters, he had already heard our conversation. "We must get to work," I said. "We have come far and have little time." He in turn told me that it was Katrina's responsibility to arrange for appointments, he had no authority over the guides. I turned to Katrina again and finally told her that I would take the car and go to the Ministry of Health if she were unable to arrange for an appointment this morning. This threat brought results. Within a few minutes we were on our way to the Ministry of Health.

The Ministry was located in an office building in the center of the city. We gave our names at the door and were met by an unusually well-dressed young man speaking perfect Cambridge English. He greeted us cordially and introduced himself as Mikhail Bruk, head of the Department of International Relations for the Ministry of Health Protection. He led us to a conference room where almost immediately a half-dozen staff members came in and sat round the table. Katrina retired to a corner and Bruk acted as interpreter.

The Chief of Pediatrics at the Ministry was chairman. The others around the conference table included a woman physician in charge of maternal and child health. She was a middle-aged woman, plainly dressed, but her manner and appearance spelled professional competence and confidence. With her iron-gray hair parted in the middle, with her sense of professional responsibility, she suggested the "eternal mother." The child psychiatrist was an intelligent-looking young woman with dark curly hair: most attractive. Others present were the Chief of Epidemiology of the Ministry as well as an outstanding scientist. The latter was a big, heavy man, past sixty, almost entirely bald; he was the only one not wearing Western dress. His white Russian blouse, gaily cross-stitched in light blue, and his long, white, flowing beard made him a fascinating and impressive figure.

Our conference lasted from half-past ten to half-past one. Everyone seemed eager to tell us what we wanted to know and we gathered valuable information about the structure of medical services. There was considerable emphasis on the achievement of the Soviet Union in the health field. Then, too, for the first time we discerned that there were certain phases of the health situation about which information was not available. This fact first came home to us in the guardedness of the epidemiologist about the extent of mental illness. At the same time we were given the feeling that everything in the health field was open to us. We could visit clinics, hospitals, psychiatric dispensaries and psychiatric hospitals for adults and children. Later in the day Mr. Bruk telephoned to say that he had arranged an appointment with the Central Psychiatric Dispensary on Thursday and the Kashenka Hospital on Friday.

The visit to the Ministry represented a real break-through but there were many other avenues that had to be cleared. I was particularly concerned about our inability to get started in the field of delinquency. As yet we had not been able to talk with VOKS upon whom we relied as our chief intermediary in arranging for visits and interviews. Katrina still insisted there was no one there to whom I could speak. I felt that I had to deal with the problem more directly. I suggested to Katrina that we might begin by visiting a People's Court. "I don't know any People's Court," she answered sharply. The interchange ended with my insistence that she take an official directory, find the People's Court, and tell them who I was and ask if I might visit.

In a few minutes this brought a statement from her that she had arranged an interview with a judge from one of the People's Courts that morning before our appointment at the Psychiatric Dispensary. At a later point in our visit it leaked out that the court to which she had taken me was one open to tourists.

I talked to Ivanov about the difficulty we were having with Katrina and how frustrated we felt in trying to arrange for appointments even with those persons with whom we had been in correspondence before leaving the United States. He thereupon arranged for me to see Mr. Malinovski, one of the higher officials in the Intourist organization in Moscow. He, too, was an ex-newspaperman and had a good command of English. I told him how crucial it was to the purpose of our trip to get to understand the problem of delinquency in the Soviet Union and Soviet methods of dealing with delinquent children.

Within a few hours he had arranged for me to see Pavel Vladorski, one of the assistant procurators (*prokurors*) of the Soviet, who turned out to be extraordinarily well-informed about the Russian penological system as well as about its basic child-caring organization.

Although Katrina had as yet made no appointment for us, we went to the VOKS office Thursday afternoon and there found Viktor Bakaev, a very intelligent official who undertook to help us in getting our appointments with the people we wanted to see. While he was not able to break through what turned out to be the worst block in our path, that is, direct observation of delinquent children in a training school, he did arrange a number of appointments for us. These included a second People's Court judge, a professor of civil law at the Moscow University who is an authority on family and child protective legislation, the director of a Pioneer organization, and a number of others.

Friday morning we visited the Kashenka Hospital.

All Friday afternoon I spent with Pavel Vladorski. The interview was held in our hotel where Mr. Malinovski had arranged a room behind the "velvet curtain." During this interview I had a different guide-interpreter. Katrina was temporarily replaced with Vladimir, who was also a student in one of the foreign language institutes. He was able, friendly, flexible and more responsive than Katrina. The talk with Vladorski was especially fruitful. We covered much ground. I was able to get from him a picture of the legal foundation for the protection of children in the Soviet Union as well as specific arrangements for neglected and delinquent children. He seemed ready to help me in getting to see at firsthand some of the establishments for the treatment of delinquent children. He agreed that on my return to Moscow he would arrange for me to see the reception center for delinquent children and he would also take me to one of the youth colonies for delinquent boys located near Moscow.

I spent Saturday morning with the director of the Pedagogical Institute and Saturday afternoon we had visits with a number of officials with whom Bakaev had made appointments.

When our first week in Moscow drew to a close we felt that we had accomplished a good deal. We had together had a number of conferences in the health field and visited a psychiatric dispensary and a psychiatric hospital; I had discussed the problem of delinquency with two People's Court judges, a professor of civil law and an assistant procurator of the Soviet Union. I had had long extensive conferences on education with the staff of the Pedagogical Institute. We had made a number of appointments, set for our later visit to Moscow a week hence. It felt especially good to know that I had been promised by a responsible official that he would take me to both a youth colony and a shelter for delinquent children.

Before parting from Vladimir, our guide, I had made up a list of appointments for him to make for us and asked him to schedule at least three or four a day for the week of our return. He felt quite confident that he could fulfill this request. We did not reckon with the forces of resistance about which we were to learn a good deal when we returned.

V

Leningrad and Kiev

AFTER SIX DAYS in Moscow we left for Leningrad on a Sunday morning. Our plane departed and arrived on time.

The Europaeskaya Hotel to which we were assigned was not as interesting as the National in Moscow, but it was comfortably furnished and well located in relation to theaters and parks. Moscow with its Byzantine architecture had made us feel we were in a strange world; Leningrad, built by French and Italian architects, seemed nearer home.

The many waterways and bridges reminded us a little of Paris, a harsher, less delicate, less soft Paris. The Hermitage, formerly the Czar's Winter Palace, is spectacular beyond description, with beautiful galleries and well-hung paintings. We sat in a bay window and listened to Valery, our guide, give us a detailed story of the October Revolution, the attack on these very grounds, the siege of the city, the hunger and cold and suffering. Valery, 25, was studying engineering and languages; he was going to be in school a long time. He loved literature, particularly poetry, and recommended books to us.

The Peterhof which we visited later in the week is a spectacular show place, a second Versailles, its exterior almost entirely restored from the war devastation. A children's playground in the park offered a fascinating contrast to the grandeur of the Peterhof. The children were healthy and well-dressed. Some of them were giving their fond parents a hard time as they ran about and got into mischief. Interesting too was the array of posters depicting nursery tales, in contrast to the printed signs exhorting good behavior and respect for park property. The parents seemed calm and good-humored. We wondered if this is what the newspapers meant when they referred to "indulgent papas and mamas." Some handsome baby carriages were to be seen. We chatted in Russian with a wise old *babushka* (grandmother) with a two-year-old in tow. The atmosphere was freer than in Moscow. Perhaps everyone, citizens and visitors too, felt more relaxed in Leningrad because it is farther from the center of power.

Our experience with the guides in Intourist as well as the professional workers we interviewed seemed less formal and less defensive than in Moscow. Because we did not use our evenings in Leningrad to go to theaters, ballets or concerts, as we did in Moscow, we encountered one of the most fruitful elements in our Russian experience. We are referring to the young people who "picked us up" and from whom we learned many things about Russian life which we could not have gleaned through our more formal and official interviews. The "dissenters," as we call them, added another dimension to our picture of Russian life.

Early Monday morning we took our file of correspondence and went down to the Intourist office. We had asked Ivanov to write the Leningrad Intourist in advance of our coming, so that we might have a head start, but he had said it was impossible. Now we had only three days to work in and had to start all over from scratch.

The Intourist office in Leningrad was unlike the Moscow one. It was a branch office and the staff was smaller and even less able to arrange for visits not included on the tourist trail. We had asked to see a polyclinic, a children's home, nursery school, the educational authorities and the police. They tried very hard to arrange these interviews. Even though we were unable to see exactly what we asked for, we did spend our time very profitably.

Edith with two Americans, a surgeon and anesthetist, visited a hospital and other medical establishments during our Leningrad stay.

I had had some correspondence with the Pavlovian Institute and with Dr. Krasnagorski, a leading light among the psychologists in Russia. I was told in Moscow that he would answer some of my questions about the form which psychotherapy took in Russia. As it turned out, he was ill but he arranged instead for me to visit the Pavlovian Institute. I was glad of the opportunity to see this famous place and to get closer to the surroundings in which one of the foremost minds of Russia carried on his work.

The staff there received me most cordially and made every effort to give me a picture of the Institute's work. I saw some of the experiments in conditioning of dogs and monkeys as well as the methods developed in the Institute to treat neurological disorders of humans.

When I returned from the Institute I was greeted by the manager of the hotel.

"You are Mr. Alt," he said, "and you have had a lot of trouble getting your appointments. I am doing what I can to help you." Surprised, I thanked him. "It is my business to make my guests happy," he said.

That afternoon I met the director of the Office of Education of the City of Leningrad and later was introduced to his two women deputies, both of whom impressed me greatly with their professional competence, maturity and breadth of view. I spent some time with them the next day and learned a great deal from them about the organization of the Leningrad school system as well as their general philosophy of education. Such problems as the pupil's educational potential and curriculum, the treatment of behavior problems, the educational programs for the handicapped and defective, the guidance of parents—all of these subjects were covered.

Despite my sense of rapport with them, I felt that they preferred not to have me visit the institutions for dependent children, which their Office administered, resorting to the stock excuses: "there was an epidemic" in one, the other was "under repairs." As with almost all the other professional people whom we met, I took time to discuss the relations between our countries. I found here again the conviction that we were the aggressor and that we wanted war. As in all other instances, I denied that this was true and we ended on the note of "friendship and peace."

In speaking of the hope of closer relationship between our two nations, one of the women said, "A mountain may not be able to come to man but men may be able to come to each other." When I left, I had to go out by the longest staircase I had ever seen. These two middle-aged women insisted on walking all the way with me to the street door.

In Leningrad I was able to talk with the chief children's inspector whose office is responsible for enforcing school attendance and for dealing with children who are neglected. One morning I spent with two juvenile police officers.

Pleasant and productive though these official contacts were, our most fruitful ones were the accidental and unofficial ones. The first time we were "picked up" was on our first visit to Moscow when we walked around the Red Square and felt that a young man wanted to speak to us. In Leningrad at least a half-dozen young men, hearing us speak English, stopped us on the streets, in the subways and in the parks. These conversations revealed a great deal that we could not otherwise learn about many phases of life in Russia which we shall be discussing.

At the end of the day with official visits over, we enjoyed walking the boulevards that crossed and recrossed the lovely Neva, peering in shop windows and enjoying the beauty of the parks. We liked the intimate tree-lined Nevskiprospekt and the visits to the Hermitage and other museums. Wherever we went as we traveled about Leningrad by ourselves we met no hostility whatever, but were treated with the greatest courtesy.

We arrived in Kiev at midnight on Wednesday and after some sleep and breakfast we had to start again, for the third time, the difficult procedure of getting appointments through Intourist representatives. By this time we had learned not to expect quick results, so after we had given the desired list to the manager, a university-educated man who spoke fair English, we spent the afternoon seeing some of the sights of this ancient, beautiful city.

It was in Kiev where I had my first dramatic tilt with the Intourist staff.

Here our guide Anna was almost the opposite of Katrina. She was married to a handsome, ambitious engineer who accompanied us to the theater at the end of our first day and with whom we had a long personal talk. Anna was not regularly employed as a guide. She was a translator of technical English. She was attractive both in appearance and in dress. She seemed very much identified with our interests and was deeply troubled when we were frustrated in getting to see what we wanted. She seemed relatively better off than most of the other guides. She and her husband had placed an order for a small car which they expected to have delivered in about a year.

Anna too was my first and only child guidance client. She was concerned about her three-year-old little boy who was being raised by her mother who lived with them.

Here, too, we met a group of thirty Americans, a university-organized tour from the West Coast. They had finished twenty-eight days of their thirty-day tour to the south as well as to the east and they shared their observations freely with us.

It did not seem possible to arrange for appointments Thursday morning and we reluctantly agreed to a morning of sightseeing.

Kiev, located on the Dnieper River with high hills and breathtaking vistas of the valley below, is a city of trees and flowers, a softer Pittsburgh. We saw more flowers here than in Leningrad or in Moscow. People seemed more relaxed. When we returned to the hotel at noon we found that no appointments had yet been made and we had no choice except more sightseeing. In the evening we went to the theater.

The next day was more purposeful. We were able to visit a residential nursery, a kindergarten, a Pioneer camp, and we spent the evening at the synagogue. A word about the camp for young Pioneers is in order.

It was an interesting place. A new group of children had arrived that morning, little girls from twelve to fourteen, all of whom had been awarded the privilege of the camp experience as a prize for excellence in the horticultural classes in their schools. These youngsters, 120 in number, were living in tents—two to a tent. We were able to get away from the other Americans who were visiting the camp that morning and we spent some time alone with the teachers and the children. My Russian was good enough to chat with the youngsters and to help them feel comfortable in taking us around the camp.

At one point the visitors and children assembled around the camp flagpole and the children, led by adults, burst into song. I made out the words "In no other land is man so important as in our land." Except for that song, this camp might have been a children's camp anywhere.

On Saturday morning we had expected to go with the American group staying at our hotel to visit a collective farm. But rain came down in torrents and the trip had to be called off. The leader of the American group sought to make a substitute arrangement.

"We've been in Russia a month," he said to the Intourist manager, "and we have never met an official of the Communist party. Please call the local party office and ask if we can come and talk to them."

The tall, slim, thirty-year-old manager said "no" in several different ways while we stood by and listened. The leader said, "Look, we've got a bus and an interpreter; we will just drive down and ring the bell if you don't want to make an appointment."

The manager grew angry and said, "You will not take the bus. You can go down on foot, if you wish." As he spoke we could hear the heavy rain lashing against the windows.

"It's a free country," he said, "go ahead and walk." Then he turned and clattered downstairs and never came back.

At that point I went up to the desk and asked the young

woman who was acting as the guide to the American tour, "What about our appointments?" I reminded her that I had asked to see the chief of police.

"Why do you want to see the chief of police?"

"I wish to talk to him about the problem of delinquency," I explained for the nth time.

"It is not possible to see the chief of police," she said.

"I will be glad to see his deputy." She disappeared, presumably to telephone. After a while she returned and said no one was in at the police office.

"Look," I said, "you have an interesting country. You have many achievements. Why are you afraid to show them?"

At this she grew livid with anger and shook her finger in my face.

"You must not say that," she cried. "Don't use the word 'afraid.'"

At her outcry a blond young man, a member of the Intourist staff who was standing by during the interchange, interjected in an angry tone.

"We are not afraid," he said. "It's just that we operate under strict rules."

Needless to say, we got no appointments. The morning was almost gone by now. We sat around for the rest of the day while it poured rain outside and exchanged impressions with the American group.

VI

Return to Moscow

WE WERE DELIGHTED when we returned to Moscow to find that the administrator at the National Hotel had arranged for us to have the same rooms we had earlier and that the staff had already placed in our rooms the baggage we had left behind.

As we entered the hotel we were greeted by Ivanov, who had just finished his work for the week and was leaving. He announced with a satisfied expression that he had secured tickets for us to the opening of the Lenin Stadium on Sunday, the next day. This turned out to be an extraordinary and memorable event which we shall describe later.

On Monday morning we went back to our work with a feeling of pleasant anticipation, looking forward to the many interviews and visits which we felt sure Vladimir had arranged. I looked forward with special eagerness to the planned visits with Vladorski, the assistant procurator, to institutions for delinquent children.

Soon after I entered the Intourist office, I learned that Vladimir was not there. Katrina was to be our guide again!

Alarmed, I went to Ivanov.

"Where is Vladimir?" I asked.

"Vladimir?" replied Ivanov, raising his eyebrows. "Oh, yes, Vladimir. Why, he is on holiday, in the Caucasus, I believe."

This was incredible. A week ago Vladimir had had no plans

for a holiday. "Don't worry," the young man had said to me as we parted, "I will make all your appointments and when you get back everything will be all set."

I looked at Ivanov. He looked at me, bland and innocent.

"Did he leave any messages for us?" I asked.

"No," said Ivanov, looking around vaguely. "No messages are here."

"Well, did he make our appointments before he left?" I asked, my anxiety mounting. Ivanov shook his head.

"Did anyone else make them?" Ivanov knew of none.

I could not believe my ears. Vladimir, of all our guides, had seemed the most responsible and responsive. He was bright, open and direct. He had seemed genuinely interested in children and warm and sincere in his attitude toward us. I could not conceive that Vladimir of his own accord would disregard his promise to us.

There was nothing to do but start all over again. I gave Katrina a new list. I asked her to get in touch at once with the assistant procurator, Vladorski, since he had himself promised to take me to the reception center for delinquents and to one of the rehabilitation colonies. These were to be the climax to our investigations. The prospect of seeing them had buoyed us up in the disappointments in Leningrad and Kiev.

Fortunately, we had ourselves made some appointments for this week during our earlier visit in Moscow. One appointment was a return visit to the Kashenka Psychiatric Hospital; others were to the Pedagogical Institute and to the Ministry of Education. Edith had appointments to visit medical facilities. We had a number of dinner dates, including one with Viktor Bakaev of VOKS, as well as with newspaper people and others living in Moscow and connected with various embassies.

We spent most of Monday at the Kashenka Hospital, observing the children in treatment, in sleep therapy, in classes, at play and in the garden. We also took time to read the records of several children whom we had observed. On Tuesday we kept our appointment at the Research Center of the Pedagogical Institute. This proved to be an exciting visit and we learned a great deal about the program for the retarded and handicapped child. We had a profitable session with the scientists carrying on research in the education of the blind and the deaf. Not only was the work they were doing very impressive, but equally so were the spirit and the professional dedication which they communicated.

In the meantime, we kept urging Katrina to complete the arrangements for the visits with Vladorski to the youth colony and the many other places that we had been asking to see. Time was running out. We were due to leave Moscow on Sunday.

On Tuesday she had not yet been able to get through to Vladorski. We asked her then to arrange for me to talk to Malinovski. On Wednesday we finally got through to him, explained the situation, and he agreed to see what he could do. Later in the day he informed us that nothing more could be done than was being done to complete our appointments. He added that Vladorski had not promised to make the appointments for me, that I had misunderstood him. When I expressed surprise he commented, "What Mr. Vladorski said was that when you went he would accompany you." I now realized that he was closing the door to these visits.

I turned to him and said, "This means that when I return to America I will have to report to my colleagues that I was not allowed to see how delinquent children are treated in the Soviet Union."

He shrugged his shoulders and responded, "You mean this might be unfavorable publicity for us. The heavens won't fall. We have had unfavorable publicity in America before this."

"Very well," I said, "your Embassy in Washington promised me that we would be able to get to see the places in which we have a special interest. Therefore, the only course left to us is to go to the Soviet Ministry of Foreign Affairs and see if this promise will be kept."

After some discussion as to whether we could or could not go to the Ministry and whether we would be allowed admission, we decided we would go. When we were refused a car and threatened to take a taxi, Katrina relented and then offered to go with us in the official car.

At the door to the impressive modern skyscraper housing the Ministry we were stopped and asked by the guard what appointment we had. We explained that we wished to see the man in charge of the American desk. After a great deal of conferring and telephoning while we waited in the lobby the official finally came down—a privileged-looking young man in his thirties, tailored to perfection as became a diplomat. We told him the story of our difficulties and frustrations in getting appointments and reviewed with him the people and places we wanted to see. The young man promised to look into the matter.

Early the next morning the hotel manager called us and said a car was waiting for us.

"Maybe they are going to ask us to leave the country. If so, let us go quietly," said Edith.

They did not. On the contrary, they told us that a series of appointments had been set up for us. They took us to the Council of Trade Unions, whose offices occupied many buildings on a large campus. Our reception was warm; six top officials sat down with us. We had tea and talked for several hours about the many kinds of welfare services administered by the trade unions.

In the afternoon we had a lengthy conference session at the Ministry of Social Security, where Edith was particularly interested in learning about the care of the aged and the pension programs. Unusual hospitality was again extended to us.

On Friday Edith spent the day with the Deputy Minister of Social Security, who is responsible for all programs for the aged in Russia. Earlier in the week she had spent the day at a collective farm and on another day visited a maternity hospital.

During the week I was able to get in a number of other visits. One morning I spent at the American Embassy going over data on economics of family life, laws of marriage and divorce, and related matters. I revisited the People's Court and thus added to my understanding of the organization of the

Court and its procedures. While here, I dropped in at the Office of Legal Consultation. This proved to be interesting because it was one of the relatively few occasions when I was asked many questions about America and our court system and legal profession. Did we have women lawyers? Did we have a bar association? Was it possible for people who are poor to get legal help? Who defended them in courts?

Another profitable interview was one with the official in the Ministry of Education responsible for establishing the new boarding schools, a development of major significance in the child care and educational fields.

Late one afternoon I visited my first and only Russian home. My host happened to be a Russian novelist and political writer who has visited the United States and is well known throughout the world. He is one of the outstanding publicists for the regime and its policies.

While we were managing to use our time profitably, I had not succeeded in achieving what had become a principal objective—a visit to one or more treatment centers for delinquents. Although I had pushed Malinovski as far as I could, had taken my complaint to the Ministry of Foreign Affairs, related my problem to Bakaev at VOKS, Saturday, our last day in Moscow, arrived and nothing had been arranged. I began the morning again by asking Katrina for news. Her response was she had nothing new to report; she added, "You have done very well."

"Quite the contrary, Katrina," I said. "You have constantly stood in the way of our seeing places and learning things. We think it is only right you should know that your attitude is not helpful to your country. It does not seem to us that this is the right way to treat visitors who want to learn about your country."

I may have been sharp with her because I had reached the limit of patience. I expected the girl to become angry, but instead her eyes filled with tears. This was surprising because she had always seemed imperturbable.

"I am sorry," she cried, and she startled us completely by

saying, "Thank you, thank you," all the time weeping in the most penitent fashion. We realized that what we might be witnessing here was the height of party discipline—public confession of guilt.

Katrina disappeared behind the velvet curtain and in a short while a tall, dark, attractive young woman came out and addressed us. We had never seen her before. "I am Miss Verova," she said gently. "I am the chief guide. I understand you are dissatisfied with Katrina. Tell me all about it and I will see what I can do."

We told her how Katrina had tried to restrict our plans and to follow her own ideas as to what we should see. "For one example," I said, "we have not been able to see a single institution for delinquents though that was one thing I particularly came for. And now this is our last day."

"I'll personally see what I can do," she said, and disappeared behind the velvet curtain.

I had little expectation she would do anything, but I remained in the hotel and every half-hour she reported to me. "I am still working on the problem," she said each time.

While I was patiently waiting at the hotel for some breakthrough, Edith spent the day on a series of appointments, meeting officials, visiting the Central Medical Reference Library of the Ministry of Health, the Lenin Library, and other places of interest to us.

Before leaving New York we had mailed a number of books and monographs describing social work and mental health in the United States which we planned to give to various groups and to place in the central libraries or agencies. Although mailed many weeks before we left, the packages did not get to us until the last week in Moscow and we were eager to distribute them before we left. We hoped they might provide another bridge of understanding. We were delighted that they were received with a great deal of appreciation by the central agencies, ministries and libraries to whom they were given, and we have since received a number of books and professional magazines in return.

It was about one o'clock when Miss Verova finally informed me that she had arranged for an interview with the director of the colonies for delinquent youth.

I was assigned a guide other than Katrina who accompanied me to this appointment. While I did not notice any identification on the building as I entered it, as we moved from one floor to the next and from one office to the next, I became aware that doors were being locked after us. I also noticed men in uniform all over the place. As we walked through a room where a number of men and women in civilian clothes sat and waited, I could not help but quickly associate their expression and posture with the scene in a waiting room in a prison.

Although I was unable to verify this, there seems little question but that the building was a prison or detention quarters.

The official whom I came to see and with whom I spent the afternoon seemed open and frank and our interchange quickly took the character of a discussion between two professional workers interested in the same topic. When I recounted my difficulty in getting to see him he disclaimed there was anything secretive about the colonies; as a matter of fact, he himself had once taken a delegation out to visit one of them, whereupon I suggested that we might still be able to go out as we were not leaving Moscow until early Sunday morning.

At this he hedged, saying that he would have to notify the staff and that perhaps we ought to postpone the visit until I came to Russia again. Ambassador Bohlen was right. I did not get to see a reception center for delinquents or a rehabilitation colony, although I did, after much struggle, get to the authority directly in charge of these institutions.

The story of our struggle to get to see, which in many ways coincides with the experience of tourists, reporters, and professional observers, poses the question: Why is it harder to get to see things in the Soviet Union than in most other countries in the world? How does one account for the general resistance to permit observation or to provide specific information?

We have talked to many others who have been in the Soviet Union in recent years and have read numerous accounts which confirm this phenomenon. No adequate explanation seems to exist. No doubt it is not a simple phenomenon to be simply accounted for. We remain baffled. In part, at least, it can be explained by the fear of the lower echelon of the Intourist staff —fear which shies away from doing anything that might provoke criticism on the part of another ministry or authority; fear to move beyond the beaten path. Even within the range of establishments on the approved tourist list, such as clinics or hospitals, one may encounter great difficulty in getting in if, at the time one visits the plant or institution, the director should be absent. Excuses such as "under repair," "the director is away on vacation," "is ill," are frequently given. All of this seems hard to reconcile with the degree of openness which one may encounter when one actually talks with the official or professional worker.

During the course of Edith's visit to the home for the aged, the Deputy Minister of Social Security who accompanied her remarked, "Now will you say we have an Iron Curtain?" And when the director of the institution pointed out that it is good for old people to have visitors, the Minister said he would be glad to arrange for more visits in the future. We believe Edith's was the first visit of an American to this kind of facility. Since then we are delighted to know others have followed.

But the problem we encountered in seeing certain kinds of institutions and services may not be altogether a reflection of the fear and rigidity of minor bureaucrats. We do know that there exists a convention or pledge of secrecy on the part of the official group with respect to certain aspects of social life. Delinquency seems to be one of those expressions of social difficulty which cannot be admitted. This is borne out by a letter published in one of the official papers caustically referring to a French delegation that insisted on visiting prisons.

Allowing for our difficulties and disappointments, our success average was rather high. In sketching these we should enumerate the places and people we did get to see officially: clinics, hospitals, psychiatric treatment centers, nurseries, kindergartens, and camps.

We interviewed many different kinds of officials and professional workers from the juvenile police officer, youth group leader, and children's inspector, through many leaders in the educational, health, and legal fields up to the rank of minister. Besides the official group whom we saw on an appointment basis, there were dozens of other Russians whom we talked to on the street, in the theater, and in the synagogues, whom we knew as waiters, chauffeurs and baggage men in the air terminal.

We also exchanged views with many American visitors, newspapermen, and staff members of a number of embassies. Thus, American doctors and surgeons did share with us their on-the-spot evaluation of Soviet medical practices; an American psychiatrist his immediate impression of psychiatric hospitals and clinics; members of an American educational tour their impressions of parts of the Soviet Union which we could not visit. Two American Negro tourists described to us the exaggerated reactions of Russians to them; a young American studying changes in Soviet textbooks on history told us what he learned of the social ideals taught to children. Many others with different interests likewise shared their impressions.

VII

Problems in Communication

DIFFICULTY IN MAKING APPOINTMENTS was not the only obstacle we met in trying to get an understanding of what the Soviet Union wants for its children and how it is going about achieving it. Having gained *entrée* to a particular ministry or institution, we faced difficulties in communication which seriously hampered a full and free exchange. This was not merely a problem of language; much more it was one of differences in attitudes, in mental and social concepts, and even in the specific meaning of words. These were the barriers that left us feeling we were not only in a foreign land, but on a strange planet, isolated as never before in our lives.

Most of the focal points of our special interests did not exist for the Soviet professional workers. To them we must have appeared a man and woman from Mars. They have no concept of child welfare, no concept of emotional disturbance, no concept of social work, no concept of child guidance, in the specific sense in which we employ these terms in the United States, in Western Europe, and increasingly in other parts of the world. This made it difficult for them to identify us and to relate to us.

We could not discover any central group, association, or ministry primarily responsible for planning for children, no single person working on problems of co-ordination and unification of services for children. The nearest over-all child welfare agency is the Ministry of Education, which carries many services for children that we would not categorize as education.

The Intourist guides used as interpreters had their own difficulties. Not familiar with technical concepts in our fields of interest, but trained to describe what is seen on sightseeing tours, they had trouble with translation. I understood enough of the language so that I knew when my questions and observations were being accurately translated and when they were not. I spent considerable time with the guides building a lexicon of Russian words most frequently employed in my interviews. As might be expected, one of my oft-repeated questions was: "What do you do with children who present problems in behavior?" I knew the Russian words for "behavior," "disobedience," and "delinquency," among others, and before going into the interviews made sure that the guide, too, knew these words. As our guides changed, I had to go through the process again.

Then I found many instances where a word was weighted with a different meaning due to variations in orientation and in values. "Individualism" was one of these words.

Another obstacle was the reluctance on the part of those we interviewed to communicate to us anything that might disclose weakness in a particular institution or phase of Soviet life. Almost invariably our informants presented only the official viewpoint. At the outset of our interviews we were usually asked to state all our questions and then these were answered *seriatim.* With one exception, no one ever said, "This is my personal view." This exception occurred in an interview on the new Russian boarding school for which, because it was new, official answers were still lacking.

The other side of this coin is that the Russians looked for official answers from us. Thus, a leading child psychiatrist asked, "What is the American position on shock therapy for children?" Our spontaneous response about a single view on this subject must have conveyed our reaction to so unusual a question.

Still another assumption colored the views expressed to us by the Russian professional people dealing with children. To their way of thinking, the Soviet Union is achieving the perfect society; the final pattern is already clear and well-defined.

Discussions about the socially inadequate, the misfit, the delinquent, the emotionally disturbed, the neurotic, or the criminal always began with denials of the existence of the problem. Neurosis, according to them, was no more than a disturbing reaction either to war or extreme deprivation, and it had almost entirely disappeared, we were told. The phenomenon of the *bespresorne,* the homeless, abandoned child, followed in the wake of the war, they said, but it has disappeared.

Schizophrenia is on the decline, they claimed, and, most extraordinary of all, no infection ever occurs among the infants or mothers in the maternity hospital or nursery!

This need to deny imperfections in the social order, coupled with the general distrust of Americans, resulted in a defensiveness which made full exchange of experience practically impossible. It meant uniform denials of failure in methods of diagnosis and treatment or shortcomings of professional personnel. The usual exchange of data about success and failure which is the common bridge in professional communication the world over was almost entirely lacking.

Statistics were unavailable and hence there were no norms for comparability. It is impossible to know whether the statistics actually did not exist or simply cannot be shared. In one instance we were told that only the Supreme Soviet had the right to issue statistics. On the other hand, we encountered evidence of lack of uniform classification of mental illness among the different mental hospitals. In this connection, it is interesting to note that the officials quote United States statistics freely, particularly those that reflect discredit on us.

A further stumbling block to communication was the fact that responsibility for dealing with crime and administration of the correctional system is lodged in the Ministry of Internal Affairs, the ministry least ready to share its methods and experiences even with the citizens of the Soviet Union. This ministry directs both the general and the secret police, the well-known MVD. It is the arm of the government responsible for dealing with security and political dissent. It directs the handling of all child offenders in prisons and in rehabilitation colonies.

It is generally known that very few, if any, outside visitors have seen prisons in the Soviet Union. When we saw a prison and asked the guide to tell us what the building was, her reply was, "I do not know."

The account of our struggle with Intourist personnel as well as our difficulties in communication with some of the officials may leave the reader with a more negative impression of our feeling for the Russian people we met than is actually so.

Except for Katrina and the Intourist manager at Kiev, with whom we could not help but feel irritated, we have come away with positive feelings for the rest. Ivanov and Malinovski represent official personalities functioning within a framework which apparently sets very sharp limits to what they can allow and what they must deny. Within their operations there was no room for the personal. They refrained from conveying any feelings or views of their own and one could not help but respect the balance which they had achieved.

In part, what is true of Ivanov and Malinovski is also true of many officials and scientists whom we met. In our communication with them we got the sense of personalities functioning within defined roles. Only rarely did the human being himself break through the formal role or get involved in personal interchange with us.

We came away with a different feeling about Russians as people in contradistinction to Russians as officials. We were impressed over and over again by their warmth, humor, spontaneity and friendliness. A few glimpses may help to illustrate the friendliness which we felt from the Russians we met anonymously.

At the opening of the Lenin Stadium my seat happened to be apart from the rest of the tourists and guides from our hotel. I found myself sitting beside a Russian couple on my left and a Russian middle-aged man on my right. All three impressed me as responsible, intelligent people. They must have belonged to a privileged class because admission to the opening was by invitation only.

As it happened, I did not have a program and therefore continuously turned to my companions on my left for information about the events that were taking place, about who won and who lost. With my limited Russian I could not get much beyond this level of conversation. Nonetheless, as the hours followed each other, we became very friendly. Their smiles became warmer and more frequent.

One evening we attended a performance of *Countess Maritza* in a Moscow theater. I was sitting next to a young woman with her husband and brother-in-law. As soon as she discovered that I had some knowledge of Russian, she kept up a continuous interchange, pointing out all the humorous byplay and her feelings about the performance.

One night in Leningrad after we had been exploring the subways, we boarded a bus about midnight to return to our hotel. We told the lady conductor where we were going and asked her to let us off at the right stop. We saw her go forward to talk to the motorman and then, sometime later, she motioned for us to get off. We then realized that she had arranged for the bus to stop exactly at our corner, which was not a regular stop.

Again, on my way home from the opening of the Lenin Stadium, I took a regular city bus rather than try to find the Intourist automobile. As might be expected, when an audience of 100,000 was leaving the stadium, my bus was very crowded and I became anxious that I get off at the stop nearest our hotel. When I asked the conductor to tell me where to get off, two families on either side of me took over this assignment and I found myself the subject of some controversy between them as to whether the nearest stop was the one before the hotel or the one after. At almost every stop either one or the other assured me that I had not yet reached my destination.

These are a few examples of the kindness which was extended to us at all times by guides, chauffeurs, waiters, hostesses on airplanes, by porters and the baggage men. They all knew we were Americans, but this apparently did not restrict their spontaneous expression of warmth and friendship.

There is one other lasting impression about the people we met which may have even greater significance from the standpoint of our special interest in the problems of children. With few exceptions the professional people with whom we conferred communicated a deep sense of their earnestness, their feeling of responsibility and dedication to their tasks. Outstanding personalities such as Professor Anna Simson, Dean of Staff at the Kashenka Hospital, Dr. Orlova, Director of Maternal and Child Care at the Ministry of Health, Madame Alexandrovna of the Office of Education at Leningrad, and many others of the doctors, nurses and counselors, all communicated an unusual quality of professional maturity and a remarkable personal harmony with their tasks.

The concern for children and how it is carried out represents an important dimension of any nation's life. Anyone, therefore, wishing to share his impressions of these matters must strive to be as accurate and objective as possible. But in the Soviet Union accurate and objective knowledge is unavailable, even to the native student. It is our impression that even Soviet citizens are not allowed to see what has not been filtered through a fixed ideological sieve that excludes anything that runs counter to the accepted ideology. Any attempt to understand on the part of an outsider is not only subject to the same distortion but to additional distortion due to his own experience and system of values.

We did what we could while in Russia and since our return to validate our impressions, comparing statements made by different officials, drawing inferences from things admitted, emphasized and denied, seeking verification from experiences of other observers and from pronouncements in official newspapers and reports.

Despite all efforts, our observations must be seen as partial and limited. Moreover, the problem of selection of what one describes out of so broad a field is formidable. We have, therefore, limited ourselves to those impressions which suggest the broader dimensions of the problem—the quality of the social and psychological milieux in which children are reared, and some of the forces conditioning individual and group behavior.

Our justification in presenting what will be a partial picture is that it may spur others to a fuller, more systematic study of child life in the Soviet Union when circumstances make this possible. It is pertinent to point out that according to all reports available to us, including information from other observers, little if any change has taken place since our visit in those aspects of Russian life which we report here.

VIII

The Broader Scene: Contrasts and Contradictions

IT WOULD TAKE THOUSANDS of pages to record all the visual impressions of even a short visit. We would like, therefore, to limit ourselves to a few of those which have remained with us and which constitute emotional links with the cities and the countryside we saw. These may help to suggest the physical setting in which children are reared.

Physically we were always comfortable, psychologically we often were not. Difficulties we had been led to expect proved nonexistent. There were no inconveniences in transportation. The Russian planes may be simple, they may fly close to the ground, but they arrive on time and the pilots make smooth three-point landings. In the three cities we visited our hotel rooms were comfortable, and in the National Hotel in Moscow they bordered on the palatial. The plumbing worked and hot water was plentiful. The standard of cleanliness was high and the hotel staffs were invariably courteous and considerate. Food was plentiful and usually very well prepared; while fruit was scarce, almost every other item of a normal diet was provided.

Earlier we spoke of the contrasts and contradictions which seem to the visitor sharper in the Soviet Union than in our own or other countries we have known. On the one hand, extraordinary achievement and grandeur; on the other, poverty and drabness. Remnants of the old not yet integrated with impressive and daring symbols of the new. The beautiful stage settings and actors' costumes in the theaters and the hard wooden seats and poor dress of the audience. The tenderness of the women gardeners in handling small plants and the rigid mechanical designs of the flower beds—months of the year, days of the week, symbols of the communist state, images of leaders of the regime. The careful, detailed execution of plans in one quarter and complete failure to rationalize procedures and provide necessary equipment in other quarters. The persistence of classes in a supposedly classless society. The provision of health and welfare services from birth to old age and yet the pervading pessimism and air of gloom and the never-absent caution and fear.

Somehow we were not prepared for this. In spite of all we had read and heard, we expected to find much more that was alike, the result of a leveling process, rather than differences and sharp contrasts. We could not understand, for example, how any of the people could afford to pay for the food at our hotels, and yet, from morning till night, Intourist hotels were filled with Soviet citizens. Nor could we understand how they could buy any of the clothes that we saw in the shops. Prices were so high for us that it was difficult to believe that, with their limited incomes, they could afford to meet them. But the stores were crowded. We went to the GUM store in Moscow several times. The lines to get waited on were long, and again long to pay for purchases, making the whole transaction very slow by our standards.

One professional observer who visited Russia speaks of these sharp differences as life behind the proscenium contrasted with life in the audience. The beautiful stage settings, furniture, and the clothing worn by the performers are in stark contrast to the shabby appearance of the theater-goer and the bareness of the theater itself.

Our impressions of our first day in Moscow did not take shape until our visit to the Red Square that evening. The gray, chilly day, plus the wide diversity in the vistas that opened up, and the contrast in buildings of many styles, all made it difficult to establish any closeness with the scene. Almost all accounts of travelers are replete with the impressions of the new apartment houses, the Moscow University, the Gorki Park and the new government buildings, in contrast to the century-old log houses. It seems, therefore, needless to repeat these impressions here.

After dinner on this first day we went out about half-past seven in the evening for our first unattended stroll—our first evening in Moscow. No one asked where we were going or offered any objection to our departure.

The Red Square consists of an open rectangle with two long sides and one short. On one of the long sides is the Kremlin, and on the other the GUM department store. At the end, almost closing off exit, is the famous, much photographed and uniquely striking St. Basil's Church. The Mausoleum, which stands about twenty-five feet in front of the Kremlin wall, faces the GUM department store across the Square.

We were surprised that the Mausoleum looked curiously smaller, not nearly so impressive or so tall as photographs had led us to expect. On either side of the entrance to the Mausoleum a soldier stood motionless. It was closed at this hour and the long line of people who had been moving up to it all day was gone.

At this time of the evening all sorts of people were strolling about in the Square, within which auto traffic is restricted. Some were returning home after work, or on their way to some destination. The majority, however, were apparently out for an evening stroll.

Since we were not yet used to the Russian crowd, our impressions may have been sharper but less accurate than later in our visit. That evening in the failing light people looked taciturn and immobile. Some seemed to regard us with curiosity and unfriendliness. A smell of vodka seemed to pervade the atmosphere.

As we stood before St. Basil's Church we became aware of

two urchins, boys of twelve or thirteen, in coarse, patched winter clothes, leaning on the iron railing. They looked at us belligerently, as if trying to figure out some way to gain advantage of us. They recalled the pictures of the homeless boys that we read so much about in the early days of the revolution.

As we talked to each other, Edith noticed a well-dressed, slim young man seemed to be listening to our conversation. He continued to look at us as we drew closer. We wondered if he was a member of the secret police and had us under surveillance. We had no reason to be afraid, and Edith asked him in a friendly way, "Do you speak English?" His reply, "Yes, I do," was in excellent English with what is sometimes called a "Brooklyn" accent.

The young man told us he was from Baku and that his name was Ovid Hakim. Despite these facts he looked Western. He was on a vacation trip after his third year of university work. In Baku he lived with his widowed mother, a teacher. He was going to be a teacher, too—of English, and he would like to practice conversation. He had learned his English from a former American from Brooklyn now teaching English in Baku. He plied us with questions about life in America and we did the same about his country.

We grew tired of walking about and asked him if he cared to come to our rooms for a visit. He accepted readily. Edith brought out cigarettes and candies and the talk went on and with increasing rapport lasted for hours.

We asked Ovid where he lived and about his childhood, his schooling, his mother. He asked about our own life in America, where we lived, and where we worked. We described our apartment, our family, our jobs, our Negro maid who has been with us for years and is very much a part of the family. Ovid said, "Give her my love. Tell all the Negroes in America I love them."

When toward midnight Ovid left he said he was about to visit his professor at his country home, but when he returned from the *datcha* in a few days, he would call us.

We never heard from Ovid Hakim again. Perhaps he stayed at the *datcha* longer than he had planned. Or perhaps the hotel administrator, who sat all night at his desk in the lobby, queried Ovid when he left and remarked on his indiscretion in going to the rooms of Americans. After all, Ovid was a student on a scholarship and scholarships are not held by young persons who have black marks against their record. We were sorry not to see Ovid Hakim again.

Perhaps more than any other spot in the whole Soviet Union, the Red Square, which we were continuously able to see from our hotel windows, exemplifies the spiritual and ideological crossroads of Russia today. In a dramatic fashion it represents the old and the new and the beginnings of the effort to reconcile the two.

The Kremlin with its traditional Russian architecture, enclosing within its walls many churches with onion-shaped domes, is a part of the tradition of this people whose history was drastically changed forty years ago. The Mausoleum and the GUM department store exemplify the new era.

With its churches and its historical museum filled with tokens of Russian achievement, of Peter the Great's victories, the Kremlin is the old Russia. With its functional architecture and the bodies of Lenin and Stalin, the Mausoleum is the repository of the new.

This picture is not complete without adding what we saw from the windows of our hotel. Beginning at dawn every day people begin to form lines, stretching half a mile or more, to await the opening of the Mausoleum to the public, which does not take place until noon. These people come from all parts of the country in order to walk past the bodies of Lenin and Stalin in homage. Their worshipfulness and devotion are very much like those of the peasants we saw at other religious shrines. There seemed no difference between the quality of their reverence and that of the people we saw in prayer, a few weeks later, at St. Vitus Cathedral in Prague.

The Agricultural Exposition represents a spectacular display of the power, plenitude, and achievement—industrial and scientific and cultural as well as agricultural—of the fifteen federated Soviet socialist republics. The miles of handsomely landscaped avenues, the sparkling fountains, the scores of magnificent pavilions of widely varied architecture, the rich profusion of displays, must stir different feelings in different visitors.

We got a sense of the tremendous power of the state and how this must influence the relationship of the state to its people. There is no question about the impressiveness of the Exposition. The total impact upon us was that of a different world rather than a mere country. The separate republic buildings, with adaptations of Moorish and Byzantine architecture, the members of the different nationalities and races who served as attendants, the profusion of the displays, all build up to this impression.

This spectacle must spur the Russian people to achievement; but one cannot help but feel that it also embodies a kind of obeisance that has some of the spirit of a Byzantine empire, or the relationship of a ruler to a feudal population. My notes on the visit contained the phrase: "the Pharaohs, the Pyramids, and the Egyptian people."

The parks in the large cities, frequently called "parks of culture and rest," represent another impressive achievement. Those we visited in Moscow, Leningrad and Kiev all rate high as examples in design and horticultural and floral opulence. The behavior of the people in the parks seems unusually decorous and self-controlled. Walking on the grass is forbidden and there seem to be few violations of this edict. The parks are kept scrupulously clean.

In going through the Gorki Park in Moscow one night I noticed a cigarette butt on the ground and no sooner had I drawn Edith's attention to this unusual sight than a park attendant came along and picked it up.

Parks abound in signs intended to achieve conformity with the purposes of the regime: posters urging the populace "to build the new state." Others portray the leading personalities of the regime. The propagandist motif may be expressed through the floral pattern. An example of this is the design of a bed of flowering plants: the design is Lenin's face.

An impression of the Gorki Park which has remained with us is a picture of the Boys' Club. This is a modest building in functional style with reading rooms and a lecture hall. When we dropped in one evening we saw a number of boys in the two reading rooms poring over magazines and books; one was receiving lessons in English from an adult instructor. A lecture on town planning was being given by an earnest young man in the larger lecture hall. Even though a number of the boys moved in and out of the lecture hall, the general demeanor was earnest and studious. But the contrast was not far off. As we walked out of the gate of the park, we saw a teen-ager, wearing much make-up and recognizable as a prostitute in any land, chatting with an army officer.

Perhaps the most impressive of the public functions that we had the opportunity of witnessing was the opening of the Lenin Stadium. This incredible spectacle, this demonstration of Soviet ability to plan, to organize and produce, was nearly worth our whole trip.

For five hours the great drama proceeded, without delays and with split-second timing, exactly as scheduled in spite of heavy rainstorms which came and went several times during the afternoon. There were thousands of performers, a band of five hundred musicians, a *corps de ballet* with a thousand dancers and as many as five thousand athletes on the field at one time, competing in athletic events or gymnastic exercises.

The audience of 120,000 was different from any we had ever seen anywhere. People were enthusiastic, but at the same time quiet. We sensed, as we had in several other situations in the U.S.S.R., a kind of obedience and control always available regardless of circumstances or situation. There was none of the undisciplined shouting or stamping heard at an American ball game, at a bull fight in Mexico, a jai alai game in Cuba, or at a soccer match in France or England. It was as though some kind of invisible restraining barrier existed between the people in the stands and the events on the field.

No liquor was sold and no flasks were pulled out. You could go downstairs and buy a frankfurter at one counter and a large roll at another.

Naturally we were interested in the appearance of children wherever we saw them. In the main they look neat and clean, healthy and well taken care of. Their demeanor on the street is controlled and poised. The girls—whom one usually sees walking in groups—present a picture we would associate with a convent-bred child. But here, as in many other aspects of life, there are exceptions: bobby-soxers very much like our own; little boys of ten or twelve whose furtive looks and ragged dress recall the "wild boys" of early Soviet literature and movies. And what was more startling to us: we saw boys of fourteen or fifteen drunkenly weaving down the street arm in arm. But these are exceptions; the rule is that of good behavior and conformity.

You walk into a boys' club and you find an atmosphere of earnestness and good form, boys reading magazines, studying, listening to lectures. Five adults, two of them absolute strangers to the children, walk into the dormitory of a children's residential nursery just at the time when the two-year-olds are waking up from their afternoon nap; you expect some commotion, some display of anxiety, surprise, movement, noise, some aggressive behavior; you get none of these. The children look up, open-eyed, and that is all.

We have referred to the decorous behavior of people in public places. Another impression that may be related to this is the few fires that seem to break out. We were rarely aware of fire engines running in the streets. It would be worth while to account for such a sharp difference between the screaming of fire engines in our cities of comparable size with those of the Soviet Union. Could it be that education in restraint and conformity accounts for this?

One sight which deeply impressed itself upon us, and the meaning of which is not fully clear to us, is the picture of women working in the flower beds in the parks, along the protected walks. One glimpses a delicate tenderness in their handling of the small plants, almost as if they were new-born children. We have been told that the quality of tenderness is accounted for by the dearth of flowers throughout the country and an attitude toward growing things which has always been and still is characteristic of the people.

Nowhere did we escape the steady flow of humanity in the streets, the joylessness of the constant scene of thousands of poorly clad people walking round the clock, walking hurriedly, carrying heavy bundles.

We have described but a few of the contrasts that surprise most visitors and suggest much that is significant in the Russian scene. The building of an identification with strength and excellence may well be contrived to compensate for the drabness and deprivation. While excellence and grandeur are exemplified in spectacles, public buildings and expositions, drabness remains the lot of the average citizen in his everyday life.

PART TWO

The Child and The State

IX

Shaping the Will

THE GROWTH, well-being and personality of a child are products of his endowment and life experience. In contemporary Western culture the child's life within his own family is considered the most important phase of his psychological development. The life of the family itself, however, is a reflection not only of the individual personalities and attitudes of its members, but also of all the social forces—cultural, political and economic—that play upon them individually and as a group. Any consideration of child rearing values and methods must identify the basic forces which shape the life and *Weltanschauung* of the nation and in turn shape the life of a child's family and his peers.

Early in our visit to Soviet Russia we noted that the guide in pointing out monuments of czars and other national heroes would often comment, "This statue is monolithic." As we reflected on what we were learning about the social structure of the country, it seemed to us the concept of "monolithic" applied to the basic social organization of the land as well as to its statues. We soon found that this was not an original discovery. Many observers and analysts of the Soviet social scene have used the word "monolithic" to characterize it.

All phases of life in Soviet Russia highlight this crucial principle and the important role it plays in the thought and life of the nation. Wherever you turn you are struck by a singleness of purpose, an extraordinary clarity as to goals and an explicit statement of the methods by which these goals are to be achieved. All political, social, and economic arrangements and the channeling of all human effort are determined by that fact. It is as though the nation were on a permanent war basis and all energy were mobilized toward achievement of victory.

How this singleness of purpose and community of effort influence the economic life is well known. What is not generally understood is the manner in which the key principles in family life and the patterns of child care and child education likewise derive from established national purpose. Soviet concepts of personality, the basic principles of education, the choice of psychological interpretation of human behavior as well as theories of etiology and treatment of mental illness are a few other examples of accommodation to a central purpose. If psychological tests disclose differences and limitations in ability, then they have no place in educational practice because the belief in equal abilities and the educability of the average individual for the highest contribution to the state must be sustained.

If the Five-Year Plan sets forth as an important goal the broadening of educational opportunity, then the necessary implementation of this can proceed. Increase in the supply of teachers and additional personnel, the building of more schools and organization of all related services can be spelled out and ordered to meet the timetable established for this goal. This is in contrast to our pluralistic and relatively voluntaristic modes of procedure. We, too, recognize the need for additional school services and resources, for new buildings and for an increased supply of teachers, but our need to secure broad sanction and approval means years, sometimes decades, of delay. Conflicting views must be reconciled and general consent secured before we can move ahead to do what most experts have already agreed is necessary.

How far the advantages of direct and unified planning and implementation are counterbalanced by weakness in personal motivation which hampers execution of plans, no matter how clearly conceived and designed, and, what is much more important, by all the evils of totalitarian social organization, is something we do not know and which may not be fully known by anyone outside the key leadership in the Soviet Union.

It is well-nigh impossible to understand any one phase of Soviet life without understanding its place in the whole scheme. Like the pieces of a jigsaw puzzle, each phase can only be understood when put in its proper niche in the total design. American and European visitors to the Soviet Union, or those who read of a particular aspect of Soviet development, can easily become enthusiastic about a single factor and fail entirely to see its meaning in the total scheme. Remarkable improvement in the literacy of the people, production of fine puppet shows, broad coverage for medical needs, while important achievements, must be seen for proper evaluation in relation to the central purposes of the country. And to comprehend the kind of future citizens the Soviet system is producing, we need to see how the national goal governs every phase of life in the U.S.S.R., and more particularly for our purpose, how it governs the rearing and education of children.

If we want to understand the Soviet goals for the child and his place as a future citizen in the social order, we must turn to the educational philosophy and practice. It is here that the child's obligations as a member of the family, and of his peer group in the school, as a pupil, as an employee, as a parent and, finally, as a citizen, are all explicitly defined. Moreover, it is the responsibility of the school and the club to make sure that the child understands these definitions thoroughly so that he will carry out the accepted code for each role.

The image of the ideal personality, which is the goal of Soviet education, embraces such qualities as courage, unselfishness, endurance, capacity to overcome obstacles, ability to swim upstream. Clarity of purpose, tenacity in the matter of reaching the goal, and firmness of will which breaks through all obstacles—these are the qualities which are emphasized by many leaders, including Stalin himself.

In an article in the magazine, *Family and School,* an address of Stalin's is quoted:

> Only clarity of purpose, tenacity in the matter of reaching the goal and firmness of will which breaks all and varied obstacles, could secure such a glorious victory. The Communist Party can congratulate itself because it is precisely those qualities which it cultivates among the workers of all nationalities of our vast Motherland.

While the place of fantasy in the growth of the child is recognized, dreams must not contradict reality. All feelings and deeds are to move toward the fulfillment of established ideals and purposes, and service to the state is to replace individual gain as a primary incentive.

In our own society, among the personality traits we emphasize are initiative, critical sense, imagination and the capacity to reform and remake. In contrast, the emphasis in the Soviet Union is on conformity and implementation. Since the ideal social organization is already known, the individual does not have to be able to build a new one or radically remake what already exists. In spite of this emphasis on conformity, we encountered a great deal of concern about creativity, and whether or not the present methods of child rearing and education add to or substract from this human potential.

This concern came out in discussions of individuality with the educators. The general observation was, however, that of course Soviet educators were very much concerned with individual development, and this would be followed by comments about the importance of the child's opportunity to choose his profession, to develop his talents to the fullest extent. There seemed to be no understanding of our concept of the uniqueness of the individual and the premium we place upon the development of the individual personality as an end in itself.

Visits to art museums in Soviet Russia, as well as to exhibits of contemporary Soviet art at international expositions, justify the conclusion that in the field of art—the same is true of literature—the period since the revolution has been a comparatively barren one. Art, as any other human expression, must advance the basic purpose of the state. All the arts must be its handmaidens. Consistent with this thesis, the contemporary painting one sees displayed almost exclusively takes the form of posters, propagandist in subject matter, intended to glorify and advance the immediate purposes of the regime. While music, to some degree, represents an exception, even here much that is outstanding in musical composition is, in the main, the product of men whose artistic roots, as well as personal experience, go back to pre-revolutionary or early revolutionary days.

We had an illuminating conversation with Dr. Anna Simson, director of research in the Children's Division of Kashenka Psychiatric Hospital, Moscow, whom we have already mentioned.

"In America," I said to her, "we are very much concerned with the feelings of the individual. We observe them, we record them, you might say we virtually put them under the microscope."

"Our workers," she said earnestly, "are interested in feelings too, but feelings, Mr. Alt, must be directed to a useful purpose."

It gradually came home to us that in the Soviet view expression of feeling was something that diverted energy from the main social purpose. Feeling represented weakness and lack of control. They equated strength with self-control and self-discipline.

When we asked a senior official in the Ministry of Education of the Russian Republic how he could explain the general good behavior of children we noted everywhere, he responded: "The attitude of the government, the people and the party makes the successful solution of the problem possible."

When we put the same question to the director of a kindergarten, her response was that patterns of conduct are established during the first two weeks after the opening of school. "The good behavior you see," she said, "is the result of the clarity and agreement on the part of all teachers as to their expectations from the children."

The two men who probably had the greatest influence upon present-day Russian educational philosophy and practice are Ivan Pavlov and Anton S. Makarenko.

Pavlov was the world-famous physiologist who has had a profound influence upon the fields of psychology, psychiatry and education. His experiment showing the possibilities of conditioning human behavior is an essential cornerstone of present-day Soviet educational theory with its emphasis on the educability of the average human being and on external pressures as a way of molding of human response.

While Pavlov the physiologist provided the scientific basis which later became the sanction for Russian practice in education and psychiatry and all interpersonal relationships integral to the Soviet social order, Makarenko was primarily an educator, but conceived education as embracing not only what the school tried to achieve with the child, but also the way in which the family, as a unit of the interpersonal relations, shaped the character of the individual.

Born into a workingman's family, Makarenko embraced Marxian principles early in life and participated in the revolution of 1905-07 at the age of seventeen. Becoming an elementary and secondary school teacher, he was called in 1920 at the age of thirty-two to direct the Gorki Colony, famous institution for homeless children. This was his laboratory and from it he went on in 1928 to apply his philosophy in the Dzershinsky Commune. There he brought his principles of combining productive labor and schooling, aesthetic education and polytechnical training, to a high degree of perfection.* He rejected, according to a commentator, "the fatalistic predetermination of child personality by heredity and an immutable environment."

"Pedagogical logic," said Makarenko, "is determined by educational goals and these are not immutable but change as society changes."

---

* Professor Y. Medinsky, foreword to *The Road of Life,* A. S. Makarenko, Moscow, Foreign Languages Publishing House, 1939.

He rejected the use of intelligence tests, which assumed varying abilities in children. He regarded questionnaires as "artificial" and "defective." He rejected "the anarchistic theory of free education" and said it led to laxity, lack of initiative and inability to meet difficulties.

During the period immediately following the revolution, Russian education was based upon "progressive" principles, as advocated by John Dewey and others holding similar theories. During the late 'twenties, Soviet educators concluded that these theories were nihilistic and impractical; the children dominated the teachers and little was learned. A radical change was then made. There was a return to more formal traditional educational methods.

"The present goal," Makarenko wrote at the beginning of the 'thirties, "is the development of such traits of character as are necessary to the Soviet State in the era of the dictatorship of the proletariat, of the establishment of the classless society."

While Makarenko was aware of the feelings of children, he constantly pointed out how their spontaneity and energy could be channeled toward the basic purpose: the advancement of the goals of the state. "Man must have something joyful ahead of him to live for," he said, and argued that "the system of perspectives" properly applied by the educator keeps the children in a buoyant, joyous mood, holds a clear-cut purpose before them, strengthens their confidence in their own powers, and "spurs them to strive for ever greater achievements."

In his *A Book for Parents* published in 1937, Makarenko emphasized the important role the family must play in the rearing and education of the child. At the same time, he was quite clear that the family alone, or the family in isolation, is incapable of doing the job effectively. Only as the family is completely in tune with the social order and expresses the purpose of that order can it successfully prepare the child for life in that society.

Parents are responsible, he admits, for the child's upbringing. But he points out that the family cannot mold the child out of nothing. The child enters into an infinite number of relationships in the whole complex world of surrounding reality. Each one of these relationships is irresistibly developing the child, overlapping meanwhile with other relationships and becoming more complicated all the time as the physical and moral growth of the child increases.

A limited assortment of family impressions or pedagogical lectures from father, he says, will not suffice to make the future man. "It is Soviet life in all its multiform variety" that will do this. So it is both senseless and hopeless for parents either to shield a child from the influence of life or to attempt to substitute domestic training for social education. "Either the child breaks out of the domestic prison," he says, "or you produce a freak."

The decisive factor in successful child rearing, according to this much respected educator, lies "in the constant, active and conscious fulfillment by parents of their civic duty towards Soviet society . . . where this duty is really felt . . . there no failures or catastrophes are possible."

The accumulation of wealth and the greed that is such an evil force in human relationships have no place, according to Makarenko, in the Soviet family. Soviet society has set the ideal. What is necessary now is to follow it. Makarenko calls for complete dedication. "With us, moral demands on a person must be higher than the average level of human conduct . . . . In the struggle for communism we must even now foster in ourselves the qualities of a member of communist society . . . . our moral code should march in the van of both our economic structure and our laws. Only if we do this shall we maintain that high moral sense which now distinguishes our society so strongly from any other."

Running all through Makarenko's writing is his great faith in the capacity of the individual to respond to socially determined goals. He rejects Lombroso and insists that good upbringing can mold an interesting and healthy character out of any raw material. He pins his faith on the rational process. He believes the right kind of education will control and harness the selfish instincts of men and that neither force nor punishment is necessary to achieve conforming behavior.

"I profess," he cries with idealistic fervor, "infinite, reckless and unhesitating belief in the unlimited power of education under the social conditions obtaining in the Soviet Union."

Some of the concepts which Makarenko advocated are clearly evident in Soviet education today. This is true of socialization, group pressure for good behavior, equal abilities and educability, strength of character equated with self-control, interpretation of behavior on a rational rather than an emotional or instinctual base. At the same time, just as Makarenko himself was only able to institute a collective living situation after he had lost his temper and struck one of the boys in the early months of his experience in the Gorki Colony, so fear is relied upon as one of the most important controls of human behavior and this seems to be true of education of children as well as in the regulation of the behavior of the adult.

Furthermore, the kind of social pressure exerted upon the child through the collective will of his peers, as well as the even greater degree of pressure exerted upon parents to achieve strict upbringing of their children, must in very tangible ways reflect itself in the development of the personality of the child. We can only speculate how these influences express themselves since no objective studies of this aspect of child development are available.

We soon realized that Russian educational philosophy and practice do not stop with the upbringing and education of the child. They are part and parcel of a broad system of social control which conditions individual and group behavior of both adults and children. This system includes a wide variety of direct and indirect incentives—love and hate, rewards and punishment, approval and disapproval of peers.

From their earliest years children are taught love of country and hatred of the "enemy." We heard children singing songs extolling the Soviet Union as the only country in which the individual citizen receives full recognition and protection. We read children's stories glorifying the achievements of the state and its leaders. "The Pioneer ardently loves his motherland and hates her enemies" is part of the Pioneer oath administered to nine-year-old boys and girls.

Love of country means loyalty and obedience to the regime and its leaders, excluding all other loyalties. Even though the child is taught to love and respect his parents, his primary loyalty is to the state. Loyalty within the family is acceptable only so long as the family's activities and attitudes are in harmony with the purposes of the state.

While it is the duty of parents to protect and teach their child, this is a delegated responsibility, entrusted to them only so long as their efforts—always open to observation by neighbors, teachers, and other children—bring about the desired results.

The inculcation of love of country carries with it, however, an assumption of direct loyalty to the leaders and the government, and there is considerable evidence to show that other loyalties are frowned upon. Even loyalty within the family is regarded as acceptable only when the family itself throughout all its activities and attitudes expresses total identification with the purpose and activities of the state.

This was brought home to us in conversations with a young man with whom we talked several times. He was a graduate of a technical institute, a member of a family in which both father and mother were professionals and which ostensibly had high standards of education. Although he was not a Communist, his parents were members of the party. When we asked him if his parents knew he had met an American couple, he said he had not told them and would not tell them. "They would not understand," he said. From the tenor of his conversation, it was clear he felt he could not trust them with this information because a meeting with us implied, in their view, a deviation from acceptable conduct.

This emphasis on primary loyalty to the state undoubtedly plays an important part in attitudes of the regime toward nationality and ethnic groups—Armenians, Jews, etc. Since the revolution there have been marked swings in public policy toward the preservation of ethnic and nationality cultures, with periods of repression only explainable on the theory that loyalties to special groups subtracted from the primary loyalty to the state.

We went to synagogues and talked with Jews in the different cities we visited. Many of them spoke to us voluntarily on the streets or in the parks. Only a few were willing to discuss the attitude of the government toward them in any detail, though more than one made it clear that, especially during the latter years of Stalin's rule, there was open and serious discrimination against Jews.

Hand in hand with the teaching of love of country and unswerving loyalty to the regime goes indoctrination of hatred for the "enemies of the revolution." The projection of hate and aggression on enemies may very well serve as an emotional counterpoise for mass conformity and excessive amount of obedience and self-denial exacted from the individual. Some observers consider collective aggression a particular phenomenon of authoritarian and conformist cultures. Hitler's projection of hatred upon Jews, Soviet Russia's upon the United States, are examples. On the other hand, in countries where individualism and individual aggression are given freer rein, expression of mass aggression is more difficult to bring about. Individualists flock apart and wars are harder to start in a democracy.

The attitude of the Soviet citizen toward the Negro as a victim of discrimination in the United States embodies a kind of identification with the wronged on the one hand and a projection of aggression toward the United States on the other.

The Soviet press constantly carries stories designed to implant love of country, pride in her achievements and proof of her superiority. Through press, literature and posters people are reminded, too, of the generosity of the state and its solicitude for their well-being. They are reminded likewise of the gratitude they owe the state and are scolded often for not showing enough of that quality.

Closely related to the ever-present emphasis on exemplary national achievement and leadership are the efforts to bring about greater historic and cultural unity between the old Russia and the post-revolutionary era. Our guides emphasized many times the achievements of Peter the Great and other leaders of the feudal and monarchic past which one might have thought were out of keeping with communist ideals.

One cannot ignore the impact the Mausoleum in Red Square exerts on Russian thought and feeling. Looking into the faces of the people standing there in line from early morning until late afternoon every day waiting to file past the embalmed bodies of Lenin and Stalin—thousands and thousands of people from every part of the vast country—we pondered whether the expression of awe and reverence we saw was an affirmation of loyalty to country or whether it was a hunger for the mystical, a desire to recapture a religious experience now past. While we can only speculate, we must not ignore its meaning as a psychological phenomenon.

Among the positive determinants of social behavior in the Soviet Union is the elaborate system of rewards developed by the regime which is based on the communist doctrine that each individual should be compensated in accordance with his contribution to the common welfare.

The quantity and quality of production, the skills and the hazards involved in the efforts of each individual are taken into account in fixing monetary and other compensation. The skilled artisan receives more than the unskilled laborer; the skilled technician receives still more; and the engineer still more.

The political leader and the artist fall into a "super" class. In the first instance the prize is for leadership, loyalty and capacity to command; in the second, for creativity, a rare commodity. The able student in a higher educational institution will receive deferment and even exemption from military service. Because those who fill posts of responsibility are subject to severe penalties for failure, extraordinary inducements are offered to secure incumbents.

Skill and high productivity bring special financial reward in most of the world. But the enormous differences in pay between the skilled and less skilled in the U.S.S.R. are striking. The bonus for over-fulfilling the norm is spectacular enough to act as a powerful incentive for increased effort. It is not a matter of scale itself but of the great differences between its upper and lower levels which is so startling in a collectivist society.

There are other incentives besides differences in pay. Public honors and recognition for exemplary conduct or contribution to the common welfare provide important motivation for socially approved effort. The champion athlete may achieve the rank of "Master of Sport"; the distinguished actor, that of "Soviet Artist." There is a rank for excellence in almost all professional and artistic fields. As part of the current program for "polytechnization" of the secondary school curriculum, a new title has been created, that of "Master of Technical Education." Soviet literature is replete with stories honoring the inventor. The mother of twelve children is accorded the rank of "Hero Mother" and receives special financial aid from the state. Lesser recognition in a declining scale is awarded to mothers of more than two children.

Fear and punishment play an important role in regulating behavior in Soviet society. Fear is an ever-present reality and punishment covers a wider range of behavior than is true in our own country and reflects more fully the special requirements incidental to fulfillment of the basic purposes of the regime.

Production is achieved not only through rewards but also through penalties. "He who does not produce does not eat" is a potent premise in Soviet life. Emphasis on punctuality is extreme and is expressed in a legal penalty for tardiness. The penalty may not be enforced, but the existence of the law is significant.

We know little about the penalties exacted for political crimes. From our interviews we gained an impression of a proportionately greater number of potential and actual offenders than in our own country. For example, it would seem fantastic in the United States to set up a classification for "political crimes of children under the age of fourteen." In the Soviet Union this has been done and children so charged are refused the special protection of the law applying to children charged with other offenses. They are tried in the Supreme Court in the same fashion as child murderers.

We learned of a special tribunal set up since the death of Stalin to review the cases of persons who had been sentenced during his regime for political offenses without trial or personal appearance, solely on the basis of charges preferred by the secret police.

Crimes involving damage or loss to state property call for severe penalties, as does criminal abuse of an official position, however lowly. Thus a house superintendent who uses his position for dishonest purposes is more severely treated than the thief who picks the pocket of an individual. If the cartoons of the magazine *Krokodil* are any criterion, such severity accomplishes but little. We saw cartoon sequences dealing with an official whose bad practices had been uncovered in one community after another only to be followed by similar criminal practices in still another industry and community.

In all our contemporary cultures fear of punishment is an important factor in conditioning human behavior. But in the Soviet Union we found fear present in circumstances and in situations that in other countries would be free of the feeling.

A young chemist whose acquaintance we made in a park in Leningrad telephoned our hotel room one evening to confirm another appointment. I thoughtlessly said, "Is that you, Nikolas?" When he met us later he expressed considerable apprehension over my use of his first name (he never gave us his last name) on the telephone. "The telephone operator might report me," he said, "and I could get into trouble."

Another evening when we were riding the Leningrad subway just to see the beautiful marble-walled stations with their fine bas-reliefs and statuary, we entered into conversation with a student of foreign languages. As we got off the train at various stations, he would move away from us so that station guards would not see him with us, and then rejoin us again after we boarded the next train. In the handsome Pushkin station, as we stood before the monument of the great Russian liberal and poet, Edith offered him a copy of *Time* in English. He recoiled with a look of abject terror on his face. "Please," he pleaded, "don't, some one might see me take it."

In visiting the Kiev synagogue, we found ourselves after the Friday evening service standing on the sidewalk outside the synagogue yard surrounded by about fifty people, all plying us with questions about America or asking us to deliver messages to relatives from whom no word had been received for many years. Suddenly the president of the synagogue appeared.

"Move at once behind the fence," he cried. "You know you must not gather on the street."

A young Jewish engineer replied to my question about conditions of the Jews with the grim retort: "Since Uncle Joe died we can breathe, but we cannot yet speak."

To many people with whom we had dealings we hinted and even once or twice explicitly expressed our desire to visit in a Russian home. With one exception, our suggestions elicited no response. This experience is not only the lot of all tourists, but also that of most foreign residents.

It was an exception when an Intourist guide did not express fear when tabooed areas of life were mentioned or requests made to see places not on the approved list. Use of denials, prevarications and claims of ignorance about well-known facts were commonly resorted to.

The Soviet leans heavily on social pressure as a force in shaping individual behavior. This is done in many ways and at almost no time is a person free from one pressure or another. Systematically built up, the compulsion to conform is consistently maintained. Among the major elements in this system of control are the set norms for every situation, the public scolding of those who deviate, and the presence in all relationships of an element of surveillance.

The workers' organization in the plant defines safety precautions, rules of punctuality, respect for the rights of the other workmen, avoidance of waste, behavior which will yield the greatest productivity, conservation of plant and human resources. The student council defines the responsibility of the youngsters to help achieve the purposes inherent in the educational enterprise. There is correct behavior for adults in the park—they must respect flower beds and avoid trampling the grass; for the children in the public playground—they must protect the play equipment. The cleanliness and good order everywhere prevalent in public places are evidence of this emphasis.

When good standards are violated the newspapers carry stories of violations and castigate the culprits. There is a great deal of frank scolding and proper names are given of persons who fail to meet expectations in various undertakings. One newspaper carried a story of a young man who, after finishing medical training, was unwilling to comply with the assignment to begin his practice in a place many miles away. He claimed he had to remain in his home community because of the illness of his mother; but investigation disclosed his mother's health was good. His real reason, says the news account with great scorn, was his desire not to be parted from his boon companions. The note of scorn, as well as condemnation, pervades all these accounts.

"Socialist competition" is another device for stimulating greater effort and forcing greater production. Factories compete against each other in the same industry. This procedure had been carried to such lengths that some managers of industrial establishments sidestepped the reduction of the workweek from forty-eight to forty-six hours for several months. Consequent loss of production would have meant public shame.

The pressure to conform and obey takes many forms. A glimpse of a scene in a psychiatric dispensary in Moscow sharply brought home to us an element in interpersonal relations that can penetrate even to a mental institution, and even to mentally disturbed children.

We were being shown through this establishment which occupies an important place in the network of psychiatric services in the city. It was the lunch hour as we were ushered into the children's residential unit where fifty children between the ages of six and ten were under treatment. As we entered the dining room we saw the children drawn up in squads of ten or twelve. A serious little boy of eight, wearing eyeglasses, stood some distance from the rest, facing the several squads. As we watched, a child would step out of line, advance a couple of paces toward the little officer, salute, report, salute again and step back into line. Four or five others repeated this performance. We inquired and learned that these were the monitors of their little dormitory groups reporting to the chairman of the children's council on the behavior of their groups during the morning.

This incident was our first clue to an important feature in interpersonal relations in the Soviet Union, a feature running through school, factory, all social organizations and, presumably, the family itself. We would describe it as a mixture of mutual aid and mutual surveillance. It seems to be the key factor in securing compliance with collective goals and obedience to public policy.

The pattern of student organization helps illustrate further this unique ingredient in Russian life. An article written in the summer of 1956 by the president of the Academy of Pedagogical Sciences of the Russian, the largest federal republic in the Soviet Union, outlines what he considers the desired form of student organization for the recently projected state boarding schools. It should consist, he says, of three constituent units: the student council elected directly by the total student body; the primary groups consisting of the different classes, sports clubs or dormitories; and a body of leaders elected by the primary groups and forming a permanent *activ* working under the student council. Says the president:

The student council has a right to adopt encouragement methods with respect to the student or primary groups—such measures as expressions of gratitude, mention on honor roll, certificates of merit, challenge banners. The council can also take punitive measures against students who do not meet their obligations or abide by the rules of the boarding school. It can reprove, censure, reprimand, deny the right to participate in council projects and issue strict warnings.

The activity of the elected organizations of the student body can develop successfully only if the directors of the institution, the entire teaching staff and the Young Communist League and Pioneer organizations enhance their authority among the students in every way.

The Young Communist League should play the leading role in the elected organizations of the student body, to see to it that the most active, conscientious and disciplined students are elected to the organizations and [the Young Communist League should] exercise general supervision of their work.

The teachers must guide the work of the student organizations, exercising the necessary tact and not permitting high-handedness or too much supervision.*

The last paragraph undoubtedly refers to the key problem which is, how to have elective student bodies and yet keep them from getting out of hand as they did some years back.

Beginning in the second grade children are inducted into the Pioneer groups, the cub scouts, as has been said, of the Communist party. A leader from the Komsomol (Young Communist League) starts work with the children almost as soon as school opens in the fall. She tells the children that a Pioneer is a boy or girl who leads in study and behavior and who serves as an example to others. She tells them of the valorous deeds of the revolutionary pioneers and explains why Pioneers wear red ties, why the ties have three ends and are tied in a knot. She explains the Pioneer salute and teaches them the solemn promise they will give when they are nine and join the Pioneers:

* *Uchitel'skaya Gazeta,* June 27, 1956, p. 2.

The Pioneer is true to the work of Lenin-Stalin
The Pioneer loves his motherland ardently and hates her enemies
The Pioneer considers it an honor to become a member of Lenin's Komsomol
The Pioneer is honest and truthful. His word is firm as steel
The Pioneer is brave as an eagle. He despises a coward
The Pioneer has a keen eye, iron muscles, steel nerves
The Pioneer needs knowledge as an arm in battle
The Pioneer is not an idler, white-handed; he is industrious, work-loving
The Pioneer is the pride of family and school
The Pioneer is an example to all youngsters.

An article in *Soviet Pedagogy** is worth quoting at length, not only for its graphic description of the induction of some youngsters in one school, but for its description of the function of such a unit. Between the lines can be seen the resistance of at least some teachers and parents to this phenomenon of Soviet social pressure:

In the large Pioneer room where portraits of Lenin and Stalin were decorated with greenery, there gathered Pioneers, leaders, teachers, class instructors, director. Guests came: members of the society of old Bolsheviks who lived not far from the school, and the chairman of two neighboring collectives with which our school keeps a close friendship. The Pioneer troops lined up in squad formation. In front stood the new ones who were this day to put on red ties. Each one held in his hand a copy of the oath, handsomely executed on thick white paper.

When the formations were formed and silence reigned in the room, the senior leader gave the command: "At attention! Prepare to report!" Then chairmen of the squads gave reports to the chairmen of the troops. . . .

The ceremony was conducted with heartfelt feelings. The children excitedly repeated after the senior leader the words of the promise. Then one by one they came up to the table where on a red cloth lay the new Pioneer ties and insignia. Our guest, old Bolshevik Comrade M——, tied the ties on the children and pinned the insignia. To every child he said: "For the struggle for the cause of Lenin-Stalin, be ready!" The children saluted and answered: "Always ready!" Then Comrade M—— said: "Guard your tie, carry

* Number 5, 1948.

it with honor, it is a piece of the victorious Red Banner of our great Motherland. . . ."

At the command "at ease" the children settled on benches and chairs around their friends, the old Bolsheviks, and listened to their tales of meeting V. I. Lenin and N. K. Krupskaya. The children sang the favorite song of Ilyich, "Tormented by harsh bondage. . ." and recited poems dedicated to Lenin while the image of this dearly beloved man who had dedicated his life to the struggle for the happiness of the people, the happiness of children, arose in front of us as if alive. . . .

There are sixteen squads in our school. Squads are organized in the second grade. In the third grade the squads assume their normal size and include up to forty persons each, subdivided into links of 8-10-12 children. At the head of the link stands a *linker* selected by the children from among themselves. At the head of the squad there is a soviet composed of five children. The work of the whole squad is guided by the leader appointed by the Komsomol.

For a plan of work to be alive, meaningful and full of rousing enthusiasm, children themselves must take part in its composition. In our best squads plans are made by the squad soviet under guidance of class instructor or teacher and consideration is given to wishes of the *linkers* and individual Pioneers.

. . . . At the head of the whole school Pioneer troop stands the troop soviet, elected for one year and composed in our Pioneer organization of seven persons. Troop soviet, under the guidance of senior leader, directs and controls the work of all the squads, watches the carrying out of assignments by squads, exerts an influence on the entire Pioneer organization. It is evident that for work in the troop soviet, students must be selected very carefully, thoughtfully. [It is not clear who appoints or elects this troop soviet or the squad soviet of five. Only in case of the *linker* is it stated that he is selected by the children themselves.]

. . . . Authority of troop soviet is great in the eyes of Pioneers. The order of influence of Pioneer organization on disturbers of discipline and on Pioneers negligent in study is usually as follows with us: A Pioneer, for example, starts to study badly, does not prepare lessons, is lazy, mischievous. Conduct of Pioneer is discussed in link. If action of link proves insufficient, conduct of Pioneer is discussed in squad soviet. And, finally, if this does not help either, and Pioneer continues to study badly, hinder teacher during lessons, such a delinquent is called upon to appear at a meeting of troop soviet and usually after the matter is examined in the squad soviet, children "pull themselves together," begin to take their studies seriously. Yet cases happen when children must be called to troop soviet, the moral influence of which is so strong and deep that, as a rule, after this children begin to improve.

We had such a case. A pupil of sixth grade, Lucy P., without knowledge of her parents began to frequent movies in the neighboring town. She returned home very late and went to bed without preparing lessons. The question of Lucy was presented at the link meeting. The girl, spoiled by her parents, only laughed at the demands of her comrades to stop her frequent movie-going which hindered preparation of lessons. The question of Lucy was discussed in squad soviet, a comradely pointing out was made to her, but this did not help. Then she was called to the troop soviet. The excited girl went up to senior leader and said timidly: "What am I to do, Ekaterina Ivanovna, I am called to the troop soviet." There were tears in Lucy's eyes. "What are you to do?" said senior leader. "You're a Pioneer yet you did not submit to squad demands. Now you must answer to the troop soviet." Chairman of the troop soviet put a question to Lucy: does she give consideration to the Pioneer organization? "Yes, of course," she answered. Pioneers, members of troop soviet, explained to Lucy how badly she had acted in not having submitted to the demands of her squad. Lucy sincerely repented of her misdeeds and gave her word to stop frequent movie-going. She kept her promise and began to study better, faithfully carrying out home assignments. . .

The Pioneer organization is the best aid to the teacher in his difficult job, though there are still some teachers who do not sufficiently help Pioneer work, but keep aloof and underestimate it. The very participation of children in Pioneer organization obligates them to study better, exerts on them a powerful educational influence, mobilizes their will, mind and emotions for the struggle for high achievement. "You are a Pioneer and therefore you have no right to have a negligent attitude towards study, you have no right to be rude, undisciplined, misbehave in class, etc." In this spirit the organization brings up Pioneers from the very first days of their entry.

. . . . Pioneer organization conducts a relentless struggle with retardation. Recently there were two Pioneers, S. and K., pupils in sixth grade, who were behind. The question of S. and K. was examined at a link meeting. It was suggested to them that they reform. This did not help. Then the squad leader together with the class instructor went to the boys' parents. They both lived in good conditions, but the parents paid little attention to the conduct and studies of their sons. The question of the boys was presented in squad meeting to which their parents had been invited. At first the parents had been offended: "What is this, are *we* called to to attend Pioneer meeting?" (But they came.) One Pioneer after another stood forth and spoke to S. and K. of their misdeeds. When the squad raised the question of whether the boys should be in the squad any longer, then the boys pleaded hotly not to be expelled. They said the squad was dear to them and promised to reform. At that point the parents admitted their guilt in not interesting themselves in their sons sufficiently. Now S. and K. have changed their attitude, started to behave better at home and in school, to prepare their lessons. . . .

I often say to myself: this Pioneer, let us call him Petia Ivanov, studies badly, is undisciplined. He must be influenced, but how? Do I know this boy? To be able to exert an influence, I must know the quarters in which P. lives, who are his parents, how they educate him, who are his friends. How does he talk to his mother and how does she talk to him? What does he do after classes? Perhaps he goes to the movies every evening or spends his time in the street with friends. And perhaps he helps his mother in the home, saws wood, is nursemaid to a younger brother. All this and much more I should know of P. and of each Pioneer of the organization which entrusts me with the guidance and communistic upbringing of the growing generation. Without this there can be no good guidance of Pioneer work.

It is very important for the senior leader to win authority with parents of Pioneers. To develop in parents respect for the Pioneer organization means to develop respect also for the Komsomol and for the Communist party, in the ranks of which they hope in the future to see their children . . . A few years ago still parents were indifferent to their children's participation in Pioneer work. But stubborn attention to the life of the pupils, care about heightening their achievements in study, growth of the children's culture which could not go unnoticed by the parents—all this exerted an influence on them and they began to respect Pioneer organization. . . .

From what we were told of the organization and functioning of a labor union in a factory and of membership groups like the parents' association in a school, we assume that in these, too, as in the student organizations, the party unit is expected to activate and focus the activity of the group.

In the collective farm, the secretary of the party unit must keep an eye on the work of the president of the collective; similarly in the factory, the party must watch the manager of the plant.

Significantly, the secretary of the party unit is urged not to become too friendly with the president of the collective or with the manager of the plant because personal friendship might interfere with the vigilance he must exercise.

This aspect of mutual aid and mutual surveillance is found in many activities for the protection and succor of families and children. Thus, if a father fails to report for work because of illness, he is likely to be visited by a committee of co-workers in the plant; they will be interested in verifying the fact he is really ill and not malingering and also in ascertaining whether the family is in need of any material assistance. Depending on what they find, their visit would be followed by the indicated action. If the family were in need, money for groceries would be made available from the factory fund.

In the case of a child who is misbehaving in school, the action might be that indicated in the Pioneer program above. Or the teacher might send word to the appropriate official of the union in the factory who would take the matter up with the father to see if he was doing all he could to steer the child on the right path. The mother might also receive a visit from a member of the parents' group who was considered a successful parent and she would offer to help in the guidance of the child. If it became necessary for the children's inspector from the school to step in because of the neglect or misbehavior of the child, he might ask the chairman of the tenants' committee of the apartment court in which the family lived to accompany him on a visit to the home. These are but a few examples of the mingling of both aid and surveillance in many of the interpersonal relationships.

We do not know how the many social pressures to which

parents are subjected stimulate anxiety and apprehension and how, in turn, this affects their attitudes toward their children; but we must not ignore the potential harmful impact of fear-driven adults on the lives of children. Nor should we ignore the effect on personality of an inability to establish a confidential relationship or privacy within the structure of most situations.

In our culture we think of conscience as a controlling force in individual behavior. Conscience is an expression of the total life experience of the individual, a product of all social influences beginning with earliest childhood, a product of all the do's and don't's originating with parents, parent surrogates, community and religious teachers. Conscience incorporates principles for behavior which are immutable—honesty, justice, kindness.

Russian classical literature, perhaps more than that of any other nation, was almost obsessed with spiritual values and the problems of human destiny. Religion, as it grappled with the relationship of man and God, with the transient and the eternal, permeated the expressions of the Russian literary masters of times past. Humor was in these books too, humor as a compensation for suffering and deprivation, paralleled by a capacity for pain, on the one hand, and offset on the other by expressions of violence and brutality. All these aspects characterized the psychology of the people portrayed in the monumental literary works of the old Russian society.

Recalling this literature and recalling my own memories of life in Russia, I was greatly curious about what I would discover in the character of individual conscience in this new materialistic society.

How much or how little of the religion of the pre-revolutionary days persists as a molder of the conscience of the child in the Soviet Union is not known. We do know that public religious teaching of children is not allowed. We visited synagogues and churches in the three large cities and saw the proof of the extent to which the state has succeeded in stamping out religious observance. The congregations were but remnants of past generations. We saw very few young people in any regardless of which religious group it was.

We visited the Petcharsky monastery at Kiev and noted Soviet citizens buying holy candles with expressions of reverence on their faces. But in visiting a home for the aged Edith found only one old lady in the patient population of three hundred who had an ikon in her room and this she kept partially concealed. Of course, there may have been others entirely concealed.

We encountered a different kind of evidence too. A Baptist minister from Wisconsin, member of an American seminar tour, was delivering sermons in a number of Baptist churches and these were being translated for the congregation by a Communist guide. We saw some of the old churches being rebuilt and the domes being regilded. This may have more meaning than just to keep historic landmarks alive for tourists.

And there are still the grandmothers who have their influence, or serve as excuses for religious interest. When members of a Young Communist League group showed consternation because one of its girls was married in a church, she passed it off by saying she did so to please her grandmother.

However, most of the forces molding human behavior add up to an ethic completely pragmatic and strongly grounded in practical values. The end—the remaking of society in the image of a truth as interpreted by the leader—leaves no room for ethical discrimination as to means. Lying, without any apparent discomfort, is one of the more innocuous examples of present-day behavior in Soviet society.

Within the fabric of this new ethic are some threads familiar to our traditional conscience: the emphasis on the education of children, on "good form," on duty, modesty, self-control, obedience and loyalty. But when we see this sort of puritanical conscience at work within the framework of directed behavior, it becomes a facilitating factor in a system of values very different from our own.

X

The Child in the Family

WHEN ONE COMPARES the rights and responsibilities of parents with those of the state for the control and protection of the child, one finds a sharp difference between the governing principles in the United States and in the Soviet Union. American and Soviet principles, in fact, move from opposing assumptions. In our own country, the right of the parent is paramount and the state steps in only when and where it has been shown that the parent is unwilling or incapable of safeguarding the well-being of his child. It is then that the state exercises its right as super-parent.

In the Soviet Union, as in the United States, the state is the super-parent, but the state sees itself as the primary parent and, as we have noted, defines in considerable detail the image of the future citizen and the kind of education and child rearing that will produce the type of character and personality that is the national goal.

While it is the present policy of the Soviet Union to look to the parent for the support and upbringing of his children, there are constant reminders that the rights of the parent represent delegated rights rather than primary ones and that he enjoys them at the discretion and will of the regime.

Soviet official policies defining the place of the child in the family and fixing responsibility for his care have been characterized by sharp swings.

Immediately after the revolution it was thought the ideal

citizen could best be reared by the community outside the family and so family ties were weakened. Ecclesiastical control over marriage was abolished. Only civil marriage had legal force. Divorces could be secured at the request of either party. Factual marriage was recognized as having equal weight or status with those registered. In the early years an unregistered divorce was also recognized.

Since the late 1920's there has been a gradual but consistent trend toward greater legalization of family relationships with the goal of assuring stability in family life. While the fundamental stake of the state in the care of children has remained, the immediate job of child rearing is the responsibility of the family, and the most important pressure for family stability springs from this premise.

The anxiety about juvenile delinquency is considered to have been the most important single force in bringing about a strengthening of family responsibility and in the development of a variety of child care arrangements. John N. Hazard in *Law and Social Change in the U.S.S.R.** refers to a study, Number 27, of juvenile delinquency conducted in Moscow and Leningrad in 1934-35. Among the findings was the fact that by far the great majority of children spent much of their leisure time outside their homes. Even those who remained at home during leisure hours came from families where the mother and father were both employed. A study of the children in youth correctional colonies showed that approximately fifty per cent had been homeless.

A comprehensive program to deal with these problems was launched in 1935. The Ministry of Education was ordered to establish children's homes, the Ministry of Health, institutions for children needing long periods of medical care. The Ministry of Social Security was ordered to provide homes for the permanently handicapped children, physically as well as mentally defective. The Ministry of Internal Affairs was ordered to

* Published under the Auspices of The London Institute of World Affairs. London: Stevens & Sons, Limited, 1953.

establish reception units and youth reformatories for the more hardened juvenile delinquent. The guardianship agencies of the local soviets were ordered to strengthen their programs; and the hands of the police were strengthened by an authorization to fine the parents of children who commit acts of vandalism. Some of the other measures will be discussed later.

This comprehensive attack upon problems of juvenile delinquency and neglect reflected in the decree of 1935 also brought changes in the law governing divorce. Both parties were required to appear when a divorce was granted. This was done so that the court could assure itself that the maintenance of any children would be paid for by the father. The amount of maintenance was rigidly set at one-fourth of the wages if there was one child; one-third if there were two children; and one-half if there were three or more children.

Other changes made it more difficult to get a divorce. While it was now necessary to register divorces and the other spouse had to be served notice, he or she still did not have to appear personally. Only if the parties were unable to reach an agreement was the matter thrown into court, but this did not touch upon the question of divorce itself, only upon arrangements for the care of the children. If the absent spouse failed to make an appearance or substituted appearance, the property was divided and the custody of children was granted as requested by the party present.

Simultaneously movies, magazines, posters and other forms of public education were focused on stabilizing the family. A light-minded approach to marriage was decried and people were urged to preserve the family bonds. Incentives were set up to encourage large families. In 1941 a tax was imposed on childless persons. Later a tax was imposed on persons having no more than two children. A mother of ten children was designated Hero Mother and corresponding honors and awards were given mothers with fewer children. These measures finally reached culmination in a law of 1944 rewriting the Code as it related to marriage, divorce and the treatment accorded children born out of wedlock.

Since 1944 registered marriage has been the sole form recognized as having legal consequences. *De facto* marriages are no longer legal. A common-law spouse cannot inherit. The divorce procedure is now focused on the reconciliation of the parties and restoration of the home is the primary aim. The trial court cannot grant a divorce and it must undertake to reconcile the parties. To bring community pressure into play against the contemplated step, notice of the proceedings is published at the expense of the spouse filing the petition. Only when efforts of the trial court at reconciliation fail can the matter be taken to an appellate court. Here, if the court finds it necessary to dissolve a marriage, a divorce may be granted. There are no specific grounds for divorce as such, only the criterion of necessity. If the appellate court finds that the action has been brought on well-thought-out and thoroughly substantiated grounds and that continuation of the married state would be contrary to the principles of communist morality and interfere with the creation of normal conditions for living together and bringing up children, then it may grant the divorce.

A husband who applied after six years of marriage for divorce, on the ground that his wife was suffering from a chronic nervous ailment and was unfit for marital relations, was refused. The court said his appeal was not substantiated by any serious argument and was prompted solely by his desire to free himself from rendering his wife moral and material aid and helping her to recover. "Far from constituting grounds for divorce," said the court, "the plaintiff's wish to get rid of an invalid wife should be condemned since such an attitude to one's marriage partner who is in difficult circumstances is contrary to the principles of socialist morality."*

In another case a man who was refused a request for divorce by the regional court appealed to the Supreme Court of the

* *Marriage and the Family in the U.S.S.R.*, 1956. An official publication.

R.S.F.S.R. This court granted the divorce on the grounds that the family was already broken up, the husband and wife had each taken his share of the property and were living separately, and the wife was receiving alimony from the husband. The chairman of the U.S.S.R. Supreme Court disagreed with this decision and submitted the case to the Judicial College for Civil Cases, which rendered this decision: "The couple have two children. A few years after the marriage the husband was transferred to Sakhalin, his new place of work. He took his family with him, then deserted, taking with him the proceeds from the sale of the property acquired after the marriage. The reason for the suit was the division of property and support of the children. The case contains no proof of circumstances having arisen of late that would preclude renewal of marital relations, provided the wife does not object. By refusing to grant a divorce, the regional court expressed its disapprobation of the plaintiff's attitude to his family. The court insisted that the parties should re-establish normal relations for stable family life and for bringing up the children."*

We could get no statistics on how many divorces are granted. Most of the persons we talked with on this subject recounted the obstacles confronting those who seek divorce.

How far the new laws strengthening the family also represent a new morality would be difficult to assess. Both the Communist party and other organizations, particularly those of workers, play a role in "regulating the relations of men and women," according to Professor Tadevosien, expert in civil law. In his opinion a greater degree of stabilization of family life has taken place. Divorces have decreased, he told me, in part due to the legal regulations, in part to their administration and in part to public opinion.

The present laws establish responsibility of parents for the support of their legitimate children and this responsibility con-

---

* Ibid.

tinues, whether the child remains with the parents or, in cases of divorce, is in the custody of the other spouse. It also continues when in cases of neglect the child needs to be placed in an institution or foster home.

Under the Code enacted in 1918, the mother of an illegitimate child could designate the father and claim support from him. In 1944 a radical change in legislation transferred responsibility from the father to the state. The state assumed the obligation the father previously carried by paying support to the mother. The rationale behind this reversal of policy is not clear. It may be to encourage procreation and offset the birth deficit suffered by the country during the war years, or it may be intended to strengthen the family by relieving fathers of legitimate children of an added burden. Or there may have been other reasons unknown to us.

The right of the parent to the custody of his children is recognized in Soviet law as it is in our own. At the present time, we were told, a child can only be removed from the custody of the parent without the parent's consent by a formal proceeding in a court of law. Whether there is some misunderstanding on the part of officials we interviewed, or whether there is some exception to this rule which is not clear, we do not know, but we encountered a difference of opinion as to whether it is also possible for the regional child care commission to assume the guardianship of a neglected child, remove him from the situation of neglect and place him in a children's home without the consent of the parent.

Extraordinary requirements now obtain for support of each other by members of the family. Grandchildren must support grandparents, older brothers must support younger ones, and stepparents must support even stepchildren whom they have not adopted. Conversely, stepchildren must support stepparents.

Admitting that the ideal family is not yet a reality, the report we have cited speaks of the Soviet family as "a fundamental unit of socialist society based on marriage and kinship, characterized by mutual love, by equality of man and woman, identity of interests of individual and society, performing the functions of procreation, communist upbringing and mutual aid . . . . [the Soviet family] insures conditions for the fullest satisfaction of the interests of the individual and for the development of society as a whole."*

We were unable to secure figures on the size of families, though we were told the average city family has two children and rural families more. With a loss of perhaps 40,000,000 inhabitants in the war, the government has had a strong natalist policy. Beginning in 1956 the regime intensified this policy along with its discouragement of divorce and prohibition of abortion. Illegal abortions continued in large numbers, however, and recently abortion has been legalized to protect women from infection and other dangers of illegal abortions.

Large families are still encouraged. Effective April 1, 1956, maternity leave with pay was increased from 77 to 112 days. Newspapers and magazines are full of propaganda for a higher birth rate. But the housing shortage, high cost of consumer goods and heavy employment of women have counteracted all government pressure and the birth rate in 1955 was only 25.6 per thousand population, the second lowest ever recorded. The lowest was 24.9 in 1953. This compares with birth rates as high as 44 per thousand in 1926.

Of course, the death rate must be considered alongside the birth rate and this has been lowered from 30.2 in 1913 to 8.4 in 1955. The population trend, therefore, is currently upward.**

Perhaps the government is bowing to the inevitable trend toward smaller families perceptible in all Western industrialized societies. The current Five-Year Plan of Medical Research, 1956-1960, of the Academy of Medical Science of the U.S.S.R. proposes development of new effective contraceptives to save women from the necessity of resorting to surgery.

---

* Ibid.

** Population Index, January 1957, Office of Population Research, Princeton University.

In spite of these swings of emphasis, child care in actuality has always been a shared responsibility. Children were never universally cared for away from their parents, nor are they today left entirely to parent care. There has been no diminution of interest on the part of the government in the well-being of the child. What we observe is a continuation of partnership between the state and family, with the family carrying delegated responsibility.

The regime has never lost sight of the many social and economic factors which handicap the family as a child-rearing instrumentality—the long work-week, the limited purchasing power of the average wage, the overcrowding, the difficulties in homemaking, the amount of time taken from the home by the required participation of parents in community activities. All these factors help create serious problems in child rearing and child care, as the government is well aware, and the regime continues to concern itself with measures to offset the resultant hazards to children. Concern about the health, education and sound personality development of children is voiced in numerous articles in the public press, in official pronouncements, and in speeches before the Supreme Soviet.

The net result of these opposing tendencies—the negative forces weighing against successful family life and the protective role of the government—is that the great majority of Soviet children continue to be reared in their own homes by their own families. The nursery school or creche idea has not been carried into actuality for many. A relatively small proportion—perhaps 12 or 15 per cent—of the children under school age receive care during the day outside of the home or apartment court in which the family lives. Most preschool children, it would appear, are either cared for by their own mothers who do not work during the early years of their lives, or, more often, by older women who take care of their own grandchildren together with others living in the same apartment court.

If we turn to the material requirements for family living, we are struck with the great variation in the earnings of the wage earner in Soviet Russia. In 1956 the average workman achieved a wage of 800 to 1,000 rubles a month. A teacher would begin at 600 and eventually reach 1,300 to 1,500; the average for doctors is 1,300; engineers from 800 to 1,300; lawyers, 1,300 to 1,500. According to a 1956 report of wages in a steel plant, the workers average about 1,300 rubles monthly. Skilled workers, such as steel smelters, receive up to 4,000 rubles, which is about five times the average of all industrial workers. Administrative officials may earn as much as 2,500 rubles a month; top officials and artists receive the highest pay and may achieve as much as 5,000 rubles a month.

Prices of basic commodities are very high, according to our standards. At the official rate of exchange, which was four rubles to the dollar during the time we were in Moscow, meat was $3.50 per pound, butter about the same; black bread (which is very well baked) was comparatively the cheapest of foods and was approximately one ruble for a kilo; rent is nominal—for the average workman it may come as low as four to six per cent of the wages earned. Potatoes were four rubles a pound.

The price of clothing is extraordinarily high. Men's suits of good quality are 2,000 rubles; shoes may go as high as 500 rubles. A good meal without liquor, in a good hotel, is twenty to twenty-five rubles; I saw women's blouses of good quality for 400 rubles; jam about $16 a quart; chocolates, eighty rubles a box. Prices on the black market are much higher. Income tax is relatively low, the highest rate being thirteen per cent.

To get a clearer picture of the problem which the family faces, some estimate of the buying power of the ruble is necessary. The most generally held view today is that it is worth about seven cents. This means that a workman's wages of 800 rubles would have a buying power of fifty-six dollars. Another factor, however, must immediately be taken into account. That is that in almost every family there are two wage earners, with husband and wife both working, and the income, therefore, would be 1,600 rubles rather than 800. One would also have to take into account immediately the low rent and the free medical care, as well as allowances for children enrolled in the higher educational institutions. Also there are the low-cost cafeterias in the factories and other benefits such as part-cost vacations and benefits under the recently enacted pension law which, in part, are available even though the individual continues working. Furthermore, there are disability payments for the mother who has stopped work because of ill-health or who may remain at home because of her children when the father has been ill and still continue to receive her salary, some supplementary diets from the clinic nurse, emergency relief from the union treasury.

The problem which the family faces is brought home to us by the fact that the cost of food for a low-income family is estimated at 200 rubles per month per individual. This means that a husband and wife and two children will need a total of 800 rubles just for food. Then, while rent is nominal, it is still an item; transportation is another item; cigarettes and liquor are also costly. It is reasonable to assume that the larger portion of the income goes for food and other absolute necessities and relatively little is available for clothing or furniture.

There are no figures or data on diet or malnutrition. The fact is that people appear well-nourished and some are inclined toward corpulence, which is accounted for by the almost exclusively bread diet. The number of calories is reported as sufficient, but the diet is lacking in protein.

What we have said so far is based on the assumption that there is equality in income and in living conditions. This is not true, with many factors making for differences. We have already noted the differences between the laborer and the professional and between the professional and the official. There is also the factor of piece work which raises the income of the more productive and skilled worker. The number of wage earners in the family would constitute another important differential. Bonuses for successful managers are still another factor making for inequality. The protection of inheritance would obviously have the effect of adding to the property and available funds for spending of legatees.

While it is hard to estimate the extent and degree of inequality which the present regime considers necessary as an incentive to greater effort, it seems beyond doubt that the trend at present is toward increasing inequality and this can be seen in the fact that native Russians will patronize the first-class hotels for dinner and order vodka and wine along with their meal. It can also be seen in the increase in the number of privately owned automobiles. As it happens, the small car is not expensive compared to other prices and many Russians have applications filed for new cars which they will get in from one to two years.

Many families are able to buy television sets. One of the "unofficial" Russians we interviewed told us that because his mother and father and he all worked, they were able to have two rooms and bath, and in order to ease the burden for the mother who was both a worker and a housekeeper, they had bought an electric icebox, electric washing machine and television set. Some families are able to obtain maid service.

Two other important phenomena add to this picture of differences in income and buying power: the government is engaging in an intensive publicity campaign to urge people to save. Posters show that the man who deposits money in a savings account in the bank will be able to take a longer summer trip, buy furniture and, lastly, build a house for himself. We were informed, although we could not verify the fact, that one-third of the homes throughout the Soviet Union are now privately owned—most of them on the outskirts of the larger cities and in the smaller communities. There is a limit, we are informed, to the size of the house which may be built. This limit is six rooms. The land is owned by the government and is allocated to the prospective builder. The government is also willing to extend loans for building. During 1955, according to an article in *Pravda,* 175,000 homes were built with the aid of government loans. This does not include homes built entirely with individual savings.

Owners of private houses have the right to bring in as permanent tenants members of their families, and outsiders on a more temporary basis. Leases to outsiders on a permanent basis are forbidden.

Despite the impressive new apartment houses which the guide points out to the tourists and the encouragement to the construction of new privately owned dwellings, lack of housing remains one of the most extreme social deprivations in the country today. The housing norm for Moscow is nine square meters, or about ninety square feet per individual; it is higher in other cities. The average available housing in Moscow today is about 5.5 meters, or about fifty-five square feet, an average of an area six feet by nine feet. This excludes the bathroom, kitchen and hallways, which are used in common. Moscow is the most poorly housed city in the Soviet Union, with some individuals having as little as four square meters of space. In part the Moscow situation is due to historic factors—the city has always been poorly housed—and in part to the large increase in population during the last two decades. The great numbers of people one sees on the streets throughout the day and evening are, to a degree at least, accounted for by the overcrowding and the unpleasantness of remaining in the home. Space is also used on a twosome basis, with the same bed space utilized by more than one person in the same twenty-four hours.

One of the features of Soviet life is the number of women working and the kinds of occupations in which they are engaged. Forty-five per cent of the labor force are women. This would mean that only about 15 per cent of the women of working age are not employed. Without complete statistics, one cannot say how many of these might be ill, on maternity leave or remaining at home in families where the earnings of husband and grown children are sufficient. We were told of women who do not work and are active as patrons of the school, as chairmen of tenants' associations and as volunteer workers in other social activities.

But the visitor is sharply impressed with the numbers of women working and the kinds of occupations in which they are engaged. Street-cleaning is a woman's occupation and they can be seen engaged in this activity from early morning to two A.M. Women can be seen working as motormen and conductors on the street cars, unloading coal trucks, digging up street pavements with pick and shovel, and laying railway tracks. In other words, women are engaged in heavy labor as well as in all the trades and professions. Within the field of employment there is no discrimination between men and women.

Women outnumber men in some professions like medicine. Most of the direct patient care is in the hands of women. Women are almost always the ticket collectors at theaters, in the parks, at expositions. The number of persons assigned to these tasks seemed out of proportion to the job to be done. We were reminded of the depression days in our country when many people were assigned to "made work" jobs.

When the new pension scheme was recently proposed, the government expressed the hope that women would gradually be taken out of the most burdensome and hazardous occupations. Moreover, women receive special consideration in the new pension law which lowers by five years the age at which women are eligible to retire in the three pension age-groups. Thus, in the first category, a woman employed in a hazardous occupation like underground work in a mine may become eligible for a pension at the age of forty-five after sixteen years of employment. Under similar circumstances men must have worked twenty years and may not retire under the age of fifty.

The fact remains that most mothers are employed and this is an important reality in child rearing, carrying with it all the consequences which may result from the early separation of the child from his mother. While it is official policy for mothers to breast-feed their children up to the age of eight months, it is difficult to say how far this is actually carried out: maternity leave with pay is limited to 112 days; nor do facilities exist in all places where women work to make it possible for the mother to bring the baby to her place of employment and be able to maintain the feeding schedule.

The extent to which children are now reared by grandparents, or other elderly relatives is an important factor in child rearing. The influence this has on the child's personality development and on his relationship to his own parents is hard to assess. Almost everyone we talked with was living with an older person. The mother-in-law was taking care of the young child while the two parents worked, or the son was living with his mother, or the nephew with his aunt. In part this must reflect the tremendous loss of life during the last war and in part the pressure exerted by the shortage of housing.

There is a great deal in Soviet literature on the subject of "old-fashioned" grandparents and "aunties" and old women employed as home workers or servants. While some grandparents are esteemed by the state because of their revolutionary past, many are suspected of passing on to children ideas which do not coincide with the present regime, for example, acquainting children with religious ideas and practices. We think it is taken for granted that the older the generation, the more prone it is to make mistakes in rearing children by Soviet goals.

Housekeeping in the Soviet Union today entails great burdens for the mother. The necessity to spend long hours in queues to buy food continues. More time is spent waiting turns in kitchens, laundries and bathrooms which must serve several families. Facilities themselves are often primitive and inefficient. It is hard to see how any time at all is found to attend the required school meetings, political discussion groups, house committees, shop committees, trade union meetings, and after-work lectures at places of employment, not to mention Communist party meetings if a parent is a member.

What the actual relationships of parents and children are today in Soviet Russia is not easily determined by a foreign observer. Few foreigners have had the opportunity to live with a Russian family, or to visit in Russian homes. The glimpses we had of young children with their parents on the streets and in the parks and playgrounds showed us more spontaneous, more outgoing behavior than we saw in organized groups—nursery schools, kindergartens, or the Pioneer clubs. The parents seemed forbearing, kindly, indulgent. Walking on Gorki Boulevard in Moscow, we saw a fifteen- or sixteen-year-old boy pull his mother over to the window of a shoe shop. He pointed out to her a pair of shoes with a 150 rubles price tag. They started figuring out how they could afford to get the shoes. I perceived great warmth and comradeship between them. These observations give grounds for, as well as derive confirmation from, the indignant outbursts in the public press about "indulgent papas and mamas" and parents who do not set a good example to their children.

We had a few interviews with parents. Some of our well-educated guides and interpreters were parents. They became friendly and we ate meals with them and took them to the theater with us. Some spoke of their problems concerning their children with us and asked our advice.

The natural solicitude of the parent may be reinforced by the mass indoctrination or may be disturbed by social emphasis on good behavior and conformity. We have already mentioned Anna, one of our interpreters. Her parents had been well-to-do, highly intelligent and sensitive. Anna shared with us her anxieties about the behavior of her three-year-old son. Since both parents were working, little Ivan was being reared by his grandmother who lived in the home with them. Interestingly enough, the boy had not yet been sent to nursery school.

"I worry that he is too boisterous," said Anna. "Do you think he is overaggressive? Do you think I should send him to the nursery school? People tell me I should not keep him with us all the time."

I felt Anna's anxiety was overdetermined by public disapproval of nonconformity.

Another one of our guides, Marya, the mother of one preschool and one school-age child, was very upset at having had to place her children in a summer camp. Marya said her husband had suffered a mental breakdown a year or two earlier. His salary had been continued by the establishment where he had worked and she had been able to remain at home and care for her children. This summer, however, she had been compelled to accept a position as interpreter and to place her children in a camp. Like any mother anywhere she was very much concerned at the continued mental illness of her husband and the separation from her children.

In his instinctual feeling for his child, in his protectiveness and solicitude about his child's well-being, and in his spontaneity of feeling, the Russian parent does not appear to be different from parents everywhere else. But it is obvious there are many factors influencing negatively the ability of parents to discharge their responsibilities to their children. With so many mothers employed and with long work-hours and six-day work-weeks, and housekeeping far more laborious, it is not too much to say that most children are deprived of parental attention most of their lives.

The new morality based on putting the interests of the state before personal considerations apparently is hard to live by in a country where living conditions for the majority remain harsh and inequality is on the uprise. However well-intentioned the family might be, it would seem the reality situation is not such as to help the rearing of the ideal citizen conceived by the state.

XI

Public Responsibility for the Child

IN MANY WAYS, tangible and intangible, the Soviet government has tried to compensate children for the deprivation which the social and economic situation enforces. The protection of children is everybody's business: not only that of the designated officials but more particularly of the whole educational system—including other parents, tenants in the same court, leaders of clubs, fellow members of the unions in which the parents are enrolled, officials of the Communist party, and fellow students of the child.

Many specific forms for care of children have been developed—day care nurseries, kindergartens, summer camps, rooms in the schools where children may remain until late in the evening, and the numerous and greatly varied clubs. There are also other more specific devices, such as the arrangement for one of the parents in the apartment court to supervise the children while the rest of the mothers are at work. Besides these day care and supervisory facilities, there have also been developed a great variety of full-care facilities which begin with the residential nursery for the child from two months of age up, and the thousands of *detskiye doma,* or children's homes, scattered throughout the country. In addition to these, supplementing the care given in these institutions, there is a variety of foster home arrangements.

While the Soviet has formulated elaborate systems for preschool education of children in creches and kindergartens, these are so far only partially implemented, despite the importance the Soviet attaches to child rearing and despite the great need for day care for children due to the employment of mothers and the lack of proper housing.

The creches so far in existence accept children from one month to three years of age, inclusive. These creches are organized on a district basis or as adjuncts to factories. They consist of both residential and non-residential institutions and in the main are intended to serve children of working mothers. They are administered by the Ministry of Health.

The kindergarten serves children from four to seven years of age, inclusive, and is also organized on both a municipal and a factory basis. Supervised by the Ministries of Education of the fifteen different republics, they come somewhat closer in their programs to the regular day schools than do the nurseries.* By 1940 there were still only 1,000,000 children enrolled in the kindergartens, or approximately nine per cent of the eligible age group. Our estimates, based on the data furnished by education authorities, were that enrollment of children in creches and nurseries and kindergartens was still not much over 10 per cent of the total age group eligible.

Plans call for substantial expansion of these facilities. But even assuming that the target set has been achieved, the total would still represent something less than 20 per cent enrollment of the children eligible for this care.

We visited a regional nursery in Kiev. This nursery serves the families who live in the region of the "Bolshevik" plant. Although operated by the plant, the service is not limited to workers of that plant. This is one of sixty or seventy such residential nurseries in the city of Kiev and cares for young children from two months through the third year. The reason most of the young children are placed here is that the mothers are working or going to school.

---

* *Soviet Professional Manpower*. National Science Foundation, U. S. Government Printing Office, 1955.

This particular nursery has one hundred beds: eighty are for children who stay there day and night throughout the week, going home for the week end; twenty for children who are there from eight A.M. to five P.M., or later if necessary, but who sleep at home every night. All children are taken home for Saturday evening and returned to the nursery on Monday morning.

We asked who decided whether a child should be cared for in a nursery. We were advised that this decision is made by the mother and it is her right to request this care for her child. It is our understanding that the admission procedure is as follows. The mother takes the child to the children's polyclinic for a complete examination. The doctor and patronage nurse, who have been visiting the family since the child's birth, give their opinion on what the child needs. Often they refer the mother to the nursery and advise whether the child should be cared for on an overnight or day-care basis.

The staff personnel is headed by a *feldsheritsa* (female assistant doctor) and in all includes forty women and two men who are responsible for the physical maintenance of the institution. Most of the staff consists of "nursery" nurses, a woman pediatrician, a patronage nurse, and a pedagogue (upbringer).

The patronage nurse maintains liaison with the family. She visits the homes of newly admitted children to assess the child's environment and makes sure that the recommendations made at the nursery are carried out during the child's visits to his home. An important responsibility is her instruction to the family in child health and child care. Her observations of the family situation are reported to the nursery staff for their guidance.

The upbringers are graduates of the Pedagogical Institute, and responsible for the psychological and child-rearing aspects of the program. It is the upbringer who instructs the nurses in child-handling methods. She is responsible for deciding the rate of development of feeding habits, walking, toilet training, group exercise and similar activities. The emphasis here, as in other educational enterprises, is on acceleration of the child's development and the acquisition of mastery and competence. She is the person whom the nurses consult about any special behavior problems of the children. She may also advise on behavior problems with the parents or help the patronage nurse in her work with the parents.

We were very well impressed with the way in which the building was organized for its child care functions. Each group of approximately twenty children had separate living, sleeping, dining and playing arrangements. This seemed very well thought through. The meals and play activities were carried on in the suite assigned to a single group. The rooms seemed to be kept in extraordinarily good order, far more so than we would find in similar institutions in this country or, for that matter, than we saw in some nurseries caring for children of similar age in Western European countries.

In our visit to this nursery we were favorably impressed, as in other institutions, with the quality of serious dedication we observed in the women caring for the children. The staff are serious-looking people, involved in their responsibilities toward the children; they give the impression of warmth and kindness. The cleanliness, orderliness and general quiet set these places off as markedly different from similar institutions in the United States.

We were deeply puzzled by some of the impressions we got in this nursery. We arrived in the early afternoon. By the time we had completed our preliminary talk with the staff and were visiting the dormitories, the children were waking up from their afternoon nap.

The children are divided, as in most child care institutions, into age groups. The beds are somewhat closer together than we are accustomed to seeing them in such institutions, but this was not of too much interest to us. The beds were extraordinarily clean and well cared for, the bedding was good, and the children looked well nourished and very well cared for.

What was startling was that, as we went from room to room, children of two years and two and a half, in groups of at least twenty in each room, were awakening without sound. Some in each room were still sleeping, but those whom we observed had their eyes open; they looked up at us but remained impassive. At no point did we see any of the awakening children jump up, cry out, demand attention, or do anything that was mischievous, demanding or spirited. It was the lack of any impulsive behavior and the degree of control in the way they were awakening that startled and troubled us. Never had we seen a group of healthy children awaken after afternoon naps in this fashion.

In the section of the nursery to which the youngest age group was assigned, we were especially interested in the kind of care given to the youngest babies. We saw in one play pen three infants, each about two months old. These babies were lying down in the same large pen, with a nurse standing by watching. The upbringer pointed out that socialization begins early in the Soviet Union and that they believe that by putting babies together at the very beginning, children grow accustomed to being with each other and doing things together at the earliest age.

These babies were wrapped in blankets folded tightly about them. We had heard swaddling was an accepted procedure and asked about it.

"Oh, this is not swaddling," the nurse said, laughing.

We asked to see a baby unwrapped, which the attendant did willingly enough, and we saw, what we later noted elsewhere, that the child was wrapped so as to restrict both arm and leg movements.

This looked like swaddling to us, and like the photographs we had seen of similar wrapping, designated swaddling in the Soviet Union handbook on infant care. We began to look out for the practice in the various institutions we visited. Invariably we found young babies lying quietly, wrapped completely in blankets in a manner we would call swaddling. In the maternity hospital in Moscow not only was the body completely wrapped, but the head was covered with the tip of the blanket. Again we asked to see the infants unwrapped and again we saw that no movement was possible within the wrappings.

Attendants told us the routine was to pick the babies up once every three hours, change their diapers, and put them back in wrappings.

This wrapping of the babies is continued by the mother after she leaves the hospital. Our guide told us she had stopped wrapping her babies in this manner when they were two months old. However, when they then cried more and fretted, she returned to the close wrapping which seemed to comfort them.

Leaving out all consideration of the advantages or disadvantages of swaddling—a subject on which authorities seem to differ, some believing it gives a baby a sense of security, not frustration—we came to the conclusion that in some way the Soviet doctors and nurses feel that the practice is old-fashioned, and therefore deny they engage in swaddling. The only conclusion one can draw from the disparity between official position and the practice one observes is that officially swaddling is disapproved but the actual practice continues in different degrees on the part of both professionals and parents.

We also visited a kindergarten in Kiev, a large institution caring on a day-basis for 270 children between the ages of four and seven. We were told by the guide that the children came from families who had more than ordinary advantages and paid for their care. The institution was regarded, she said, as a model one.

The approach was through a superbly kept park-like area. The buildings were brick and well-kept. Inside, we were struck by the impressive staircases, the spaciousness of the rooms and the beautiful polished floors. As we went from one immaculate room to the next we could not conceal our surprise that an institution for children should present such a spotless appearance. We did not see how it could possibly be in active use for the purpose it was supposed to serve. Several times we asked our guide and members of the staff if these were the rooms in which children lived, napped and played. Each time we were assured they were.

In each of the large playrooms dozens of toys and dolls and

teddy bears were set up on display. Each of us walked over and examined these toys and the meticulous manner in which they were arranged, and were not surprised, as we picked up one after another, to find that they looked unused. We asked our guide, herself the mother of a young child, and a particularly friendly person, whether it was possible the children had had anything to do with these displays. She tactfully posed the question to one of the teachers. We were assured this was indeed the work of the children, they had arranged the display for us.

"But," Edith persisted, "how *could* four- or five-year-old children have done this?"

The teacher smiled and bobbed her head. "Oh yes," she said, "the children enjoyed doing this for you." Evidently she felt our amazement was a tribute to the precociousness and social sense of Russian children. One could not help but wonder if the children had ever played with these toys.

A similar quality of newness was apparent in the furnishings of the dormitories used by the children for rest periods. Embroidered pillow slips, counterpanes and all manner of freshly starched linens and laces embellished the place. It was in no way clear to us how a large children's institution could retain this appearance and still function without excessive restraint of its young inhabitants.

Our guide, a natural, direct person, was troubled by our reactions. Finally she said: "Maybe they have fixed it up for the visit, but wouldn't you do the same?"

We saw no signs of the sand and water play apparatus or building toys found in American kindergartens and no indications of painting or drawing activity. When we kept pressing various people for some explanation of the freshly varnished floors and the lack of any sign that the rooms were being used by children, they finally said, "Well, this is summer time and the children are out of doors all day."

Despite earlier rain, the day had turned out beautiful, the sun was shining, and the children were working, studying and playing in small groups in the spacious grounds. Fine fruit trees and delightful walks were interspersed with elaborate flower beds arranged in great precision. Again we were told the children themselves had planted and tended these flowers, and again it was hard to believe. The boys and girls were playing, laughing and listening to teachers tell stories, and seemed unrestrained, free and enjoying themselves.

At five o'clock these youngsters who had been in the kindergarten since eight o'clock in the morning prepared to go home. We followed them to the locker rooms. As they moved about, changing their clothes, sitting on the benches, putting on their shoes, we were struck by the absence of any of the jostling and horseplay seen at home under similar circumstances. Only occasionally did a child give another a poke and when he did it was a very gentle poke.

We commented to the director on this perfect conformity of behavior.

"But *some* children must misbehave," we said. "What do you do with them?"

She pointed out one little boy who was meticulously folding his uniform and putting it in his locker.

"At the beginning of the term," she said, "Boris was rebellious, disobedient and destructive. We gave him jobs we knew would interest him and brought up his status and prestige in the eyes of the other children."

Again and again we met with an overrational common-sense attitude. There was no probing into possible causes, as to how a child might be feeling; there were just matter-of-fact "sensible" methods based on social approval.

As compared to the United States and Western Europe, Soviet Russia has developed fewer specialized facilities for aid to families and children facing serious problems which threaten the integrity of the family or the health and well-being of the child. There are two social factors, one of which would appear to limit the development of such services, the other to enlarge it.

The premise that the social order is approaching a level of perfection would tend to decrease the need as well as the importance of specialized remedial and protective services. At the same time, some of the economic and social factors influencing family life, such as overcrowding and employment of mothers, emphasize the need for a greater degree of protection. The jeopardy to children which stems from the inability of parents to provide as much supervision as desired has been met, as will be seen in our report, through the broadening of the scope of responsibility of the educational and health authorities as well as the mutual aid activities of other groups.

Four ministries have an important role in providing specialized service to children. The two which, we believe, carry the greatest amount of responsibility are the Ministries of Health and Education. A more limited responsibility is carried by the Ministries of Internal Affairs and Social Security. The varied health, welfare and educational services carried by the labor unions not only supplement those provided by the ministries, but include many distinct services by themselves.

The republic ministries of health provide universal health coverage for all human beings from infancy through adulthood, both general and specialized service, through outpatient clinics as well as through a variety of specialized hospital and institutional facilities. In addition to the provision of medical care, the health program expresses more fully than is true in our own country the interest of the state in the health of the individual. The protection of the young child is not left to chance or to the will of the mother; homes are routinely visited and the mother is required to bring the child to the clinic. Furthermore, the scope of responsibility of the health authority is very broad and includes not only health care, but health education and some dietary and other financial assistance. As we have already reported, the nurseries, both day and residential, are under the direct supervision of the health authority.

As is true in the case of the health authority, the education authorities carry many responsibilities for children beyond that of providing formal schooling. If we were to select one department as the chief protective agency for children, it would be the educational ministry. Beyond education in the usual sense, the educational authorities provide a variety of specific and general protective services for children. Child protection, child placement, foster home and institutional care for the neglected child are a few examples of the specific child care functions carried on by the educational authorities.

The Ministry of Internal Affairs provides special services to children through the juvenile police officer and also administers youth reformatories or colonies for delinquent children. The Ministry of Social Security is responsible for residential care of imbecile and idiot children as well as some classes of physically handicapped.

Volunteers have an important part in the provision of social services to people in the Soviet Union. This is best exemplified in the many kinds of responsibilities which members of the special union committees carry. There seems to be a great deal of participation by a great number of people in a variety of forms of mutual aid.

It is beyond our special interest to undertake any description of the total function of the labor union in Soviet society today. We did have the opportunity of a very full discussion with leaders in the All-Soviet Council of Trade Unions and gained from them some idea of the functions of this important organization.

The Russian trade union plays an active part both in protection of workers and in building the economic structure of the state. According to the Council officials, not a single law affecting labor is adopted without participation by the trade union organization. They claimed that they had an active part in working out recent laws which have the effect of changing the rates of pay.

The membership of the trade unions within the Soviet Union has reached a total of 40,000,000 workers. It includes most of the employed in the population with the exception of collective farmers and self-employed. Membership in the union is voluntary, although over ninety per cent of the workmen belong;

since it is so clearly in the interest of each person to join, the difference between the total number of workmen and those enrolled largely represents a lag in the process of the enrollment itself. The structure of trade unions is that of a pyramid, with the local factory unit constituting the base; you then work upward through the city unit, regional unit, republic unit, to the All-Union federation.

We are not in a position to assess how far the trade union in Soviet Russia exists in order to advance the interests of its members, or how far it represents an arm of the government through which it deals with problems of labor. What we are clear about is that the labor union plays an important part in lives of the people. Outside the government itself, it is one of the most important agencies serving as a protective mutual aid association. The labor union carries many responsibilities affecting the daily lives of the average individual. Thus, at every level of organization, from the plant up through the central federation, there exist a number of commissions concerned with such problems as housing and welfare, health, safety, vacations and annual leaves; wages, general education; children's work; social insurance.

We were told that 1,250,000 workers were active in the field of housing and welfare. All these participants receive special instructions on how to organize this activity. In each plant, the Housing and Welfare Committee works closely with the Committee on Cafeterias and Nutrition. Much of the construction and management of public housing is closely connected with the operation of the plant, and, except in some of the larger cities like Moscow, Kiev and Leningrad, much of the housing is directly built by the plant, rather than the municipality.

It is also usual for the plant to advance loans to workers who wish to build their own homes. The trade union committee is responsible not only for the supervision of the building of houses and assistance to individuals who wish to build houses, but also carries the direct task of assigning flats in newly-built apartment houses.

The union also operates the cafeterias in the plants. These

are under the supervision of a union committee which sets the prices and the portions, and also watches over the standards of service. The prices are low because of the free transportation and free buildings provided. They told us that meals in the plants might be as low as one and a half to two rubles for lunch, and only twenty-five kopeks for tea. It is also possible for women workers to take home a cooked dinner from the factory dining room.

The Committee on Children's Work is concerned with the maintenance of the children's nursery and also, in some instances, the kindergartens. The Committee on Social Insurance, which covers primarily disability and sick benefits, is also administered by the plant. Approximately nine per cent of the total payroll is deposited in the social insurance fund. In addition to sick benefits, the admissions to sanatoria are also determined by committees of the union. One-fourth of these admissions are entirely free, others involve a part-payment by the worker and a seventy per cent payment by the union. It is also possible for the union to provide special nourishment for the worker. In the case of illness, the salary will continue even though the worker is home ill.

A statement summarizing the responsibilities of a plant trade union committee is contained in the report entitled *Labour Protection at Soviet Industrial Enterprises*:

> With a view to ensuring improved working conditions and rest facilities for the workers, engineering and technical staff and office personnel, the plant trade union committee undertakes:
>
> a) to effect systematic control over the operation of the labour legislation relating to working hours and rest periods, the provision of current and extra vacations for all employees, according to the timetable adopted, and with the provision of the rebates and privileges established for juveniles, pregnant women and nursing mothers;
>
> b) to keep a systematic check on the working conditions in the shops and departments, and on the fulfilment [sic] of the agreement for ameliorating working conditions and of the factory regulations;
>
> c) to keep a systematic check to ensure that the workers are

supplied in good time with good-quality working clothes, boots and soap, and also milk and butter in the standard quantities;

d) to engage in systematic explanatory work among the employees aimed at averting accidents and sickness, periodically to discuss problems concerning the protection of labour, safety-first measures and industrial hygiene at meetings of shop committees, and of labour protection commissions, and at meetings of the plant trade union committee;

e) to send 460 employees to holiday homes or sanatoria during 1952;

f) to arrange for not less than 600 employees to attend the night sanatorium during the year; the management undertakes to ensure the timely repair of the sanatorium premises, the provision of equipment, of lighting, heating, and transport facilities, and also to see to the cleanliness and security of the buildings;

g) to allocate the sum of 60,000 rubles to enable workers and members of the engineering and technical staff to secure special diets at reduced rates;

h) to arrange systematic assistance for employees lying ill at home.

Analysis of the foregoing summary of some of the responsibilities which are carried by the trade unions reveals that many of them would in our own country be the responsibility of local, state or federal government. It also indicates the tremendous meaning which the trade union and the plant itself have in the lives of the workmen. The union is not only the source of livelihood but also determines many phases of a member's housing arrangement, his own vocational education, his recreational plans, such as summer vacations, his medical care, his insurance and also his club. If the workmen participate in any degree consistent with all the tasks that are assigned, then many of them must devote a good deal of their leisure time to the sponsorship and supervision and management of the non-industrial activities which the union maintains.

There is no concept of professional social work as a philosophy and method of helping individuals in difficulty, and therefore there is no concept of the social worker and no social work profession in the Soviet Union. Functions usually identified with social work and child welfare are provided by a number of different professional workers, as well as volunteers.

The patronage nurse working out of a clinic, residential nursery or nursery school, or a maternity hospital, carries some of the responsibilities which in our country are carried by the family or psychiatric caseworker, or the visiting nurse. She not only helps parents to meet health problems, she also assesses the ability of parents to carry out an environmental program for the disturbed child. In the case of a child coming to the nursery, it is she who is responsible for helping the parents in sound arrangements for the child when he is at home.

The teacher is not only responsible for education, but is also one of the persons to whom parents may turn for advice on child behavior and child guidance.

A more specialized worker is the upbringer, who serves, as we noted earlier, as professional counselor in the institution. He is usually, although not always, a teacher by training. It is he who is responsible for dealing with the more personal psychological conflicts of the child.

The work of the children's inspector comes closest to that of certain child welfare functions in our own country. He works closely with the school; he is responsible for dealing with nonattendance and behavior problems; he is the one who investigates complaints of neglect; he also supervises placement of children in foster homes.

The children's police are responsible for dealing with runaway children, milder cases of delinquency. We learned of one other professional person who may be said to carry social welfare functions. He is the advocate of the People's Court, serving as a member of the staff of the family legal consultation service attached to the People's Court. This probably comes closer to the legal aid function as we know it in our own country.

It is significant that neither the patronage nurse nor the children's inspector, the upbringer nor the juvenile police receive any specialized training for their responsibilities. The nurse has been trained as a nurse; the children's inspector has usually been trained as a teacher, but has had no training beyond that for his specialized child care protective responsibilities; the doctor in charge is a general practitioner or specialist, depending on the character of the health institution.

In different ways advice and help in child guidance are given to parents. A parent who is troubled about the progress his child is making or about difficulties in behavior may turn to a number of different professions or agencies. She may go to the polyclinics where the problem may be referred to the neurologist-psychiatrists. She may go to the teacher of the child or to the principal of the school. She may also go to the party unit to which she belongs or to the trade union of which she or her husband is a member. Child guidance as a specialized function in the sense in which it exists in our country is not known in the Soviet Union.

As we shall see in our consideration of the services for mentally ill and delinquent children, while no formal case-study procedures in the comprehensive sense in which we have come to know them are available to children in the Soviet, a considerable amount of careful study appears to be given to behavior problems and learning problems. Not only are physical and medical examinations given to the child, but an attempt is made to gather a history of the whole situation involving the attitudes of parents. This is done in the psychiatric clinics. In an informal way it is also done by the teacher. In the cases of retarded children, the teacher, the doctor, and the psychologist all participate in observation and assessment of the problem.

Our impression is that in the main parents will turn to the teacher for help on most of the problems which we would consider behavior problems. The teacher, in turn, relies on environmental changes, on encouragement, on scolding, on changes in the child's educational program, on advice to parents. If the efforts of teacher, clinic, other students, other parents, fail to bring about any significant improvement in the situation and the child continues to present serious behavior problems within the school or within the community, the educational authorities together with the doctor will decide on the placement of the child in the disciplinary school under the direction of the local educational authorities. The programs of these disciplinary schools are briefly described in the chapter dealing with the treatment of delinquent children.

Complaints about the neglect of children are filed with the school authorities and become the special province of the children's inspector. One or more officials of this kind are employed in each district in cities like Leningrad and Moscow. They are the workers especially responsible for child protection and child care. Assuming that all other kinds of social pressures upon the parents and the child have been exercised and proved of no avail, the children's inspector may file a complaint in the People's Court charging the parent with neglect. The court may decide to fine or otherwise punish the parent, and may also decide to remove the child, if it is in the child's best interest, from the care and custody of the parent.

The local soviet in urban or rural communities is the basic guardianship agency and carries responsibility for the care of children entrusted to it by the courts. It may delegate this responsibility to a children's commission and to appropriate ministries—i.e., Health, Education and Social Security. How far the local soviet or the children's commission which it has established may on its own initiative take action to protect neglected children is not clear. While there is no question that it may assume responsibility for children upon the death of their parents, and may also intervene to protect the child pending court action against the parents, it is not clear whether it has the right to assume custody on any permanent basis without the consent of the parents, or force placement of the child against the wishes of the parents. The weight of what was reported to us would indicate that it does not have that right; this can only be accomplished through court action.

In our interviews with a children's inspector and with a

number of school authorities, we tried to discover what their attitudes were toward the removal of children. We wanted to find out how much importance was given to keeping the child in his own home, or to the principle that it is best under most circumstances for children to remain with their own parents. The answers in response to this question were usually an affirmation of this principle. This, however, is contradicted by the views expressed by a number of educators that the educator is much more qualified to take care of children than are the child's own parents.

Our interviews and observational visits during our stay in Soviet Russia did not disclose the extent of the care of children away from their own families. In the United States approximately two hundred thousand children are cared for outside of their own homes. There are no facts to indicate whether or not the number of children living under these circumstances is greater in the Soviet Union than in our own country. But there are many reasons why one might assume that the number is much greater. Some of the facts reported here, as well as others we are about to refer to, would seem to substantiate the conclusion that the number of such children is many times greater. The employment of women, the number of children and others living in incomplete families—partly due to the loss of fathers in the war—the overcrowding are but a few of the factors that contribute to the placement of children.

If we turn to more specific indices, we find that in a city like Kiev there were at the time of our visit sixty-seven residential nurseries with an aggregate approximate population of over 7,000, serving children from two months to three years. In Leningrad, the Board of Education administers fifty children's home for school-age children and fourteen for the kindergarten-age level. This does not include the two disciplinary schools with 300 children in each, nor does it include the residential children's nurseries. In addition, we learned that there are approximately 300 to 600 children in each of the 15 regions in the city of Leningrad placed in foster homes.

There are also psychological factors which would point to a much greater reliance upon substitute home facilities. For one example, the anxiety about neglect, which one encounters in talks with all professional people. For another example, the confidence that the professional pedagogue and the nurse can give children better care than most parents.

What we have described may constitute a basis for the assumption that a substantial proportion of all children are cared for outside of their own families—approximately what percentage we do not know.

Three types of foster home placement are in effect at the present time: adoption, guardianship and the *patronat* or patronage home. The legal provisions for adoption have been part of Soviet law since 1926. They followed a period of eight years during which adoption had been prohibited. John Hazard in his book, *Law and Social Change in the U.S.S.R.,** cites the following reasons:

(1) adoption was thought to be an institution used under bourgeois law as a means for the exploitation of children:
(2) mass institutional care of children was expected to develop so rapidly that the homeless waif would not require a foster home: and
(3) the draftsmen of the 1918 Family Code wished to avoid all possibility of violation of their policy against inheritance as it then existed. Adoption would have permitted outsiders to qualify under the one exception authorising members of the family to keep the immediate chattels of the deceased if they did not exceed in value 10,000 rubles.

The provisions for adoption are not substantially different from our own: only persons under eighteen can be adopted; consent of living parents must be obtained except where parents have been deprived of legal rights; if the child is over ten, his consent must be obtained. Those applying for adoption must establish their character and prove that their interests are not in conflict with the interests of the child. It is also possible after adoption, under exceptional circumstances, to

* Pp. 257-259.

have the adoption set aside. Adoption has to be approved by the guardianship agency of the local soviet and as a step to final registration. The adopted child has the same duties and rights of a natural child, including the right of inheritance and maintenance.

While there was no reference to this in our interviews, we have learned from reading that there is another status, an interesting variation of the institution of adoption; this is dependency, in existence since 1928. This status differs from that of adoption in that it does not carry a change of name, inheritance rights and support. It is both less than adoption and more than guardianship and carries with it many of the same conditions as our indenture arrangement. The person who has taken the child into his home as a dependent is bound to continue to provide care for him so long as he remains a minor and is unable to work.

The *patronat* comes closest to our ordinary foster boarding home. Under this law, enacted in 1936, a person might take a child between the ages of five months and fourteen years into his home under contract. If the child is under four, the contract is with the Ministry of Health; if he is over four, the contract is with the Ministry of Education. The relationship continues until he is sixteen. The *patron*, or foster parent, is paid monthly by the contracting agency. The responsibilities of the foster family have been spelled out in the law and are, in general, those of a legal custodian.

XII

Health Services

HEALTH SERVICES and medical care are everywhere recognized as crucial factors in the maintenance of individual and family well-being. The extent and quality of public protection of human resources within the Soviet social policy are exemplified in the free universal health care provided by the constitution for all citizens from birth to death. Moreover, the interest of the state in the health of each individual adds a special dimension to these services. The protection of the young child is not left to chance or to the whim of the parents. Homes are routinely visited and a mother is required to bring her child to the district polyclinic.

Reports on the medical care program of the Soviet Union were published in Europe and the United States during the 'thirties and 'forties, but few firsthand observations have come to us in the last ten years. Recent liberalization of travel is at last making it possible for foreign experts to see how this vast program of free medical service works. It is the first look at a comprehensive solution to a problem increasingly burdensome to all the countries of the world.

The description of the Soviet plan of health services was set forth in 1947 by a distinguished medical historian,* but many wondered as time went on if his description still applied, or if there were changes and in what direction.

---

* Henry E. Sigerist, *Medicine and Health in the Soviet Union.* New York: Citadel Press, 1947.

What is the present scope of the Soviet Union's free medical care services? How can the government administer a health program for a population of two hundred million, living in fifteen different republics, embracing people who, we may assume, have different attitudes toward illness, toward doctors, and toward measures required for maintenance of their health and that of their children? What type of professional workers are involved in giving medical care and what kind of training do they receive? Does the Soviet Union have the problem of shortages of health personnel that we face so acutely in our country? How does medical practice differ from medical practice in our country? How do medical care facilities compare with ours? What is the character of the relationship between doctors and patients? Does private medical practice exist in the Soviet Union?

What follows is not intended to be a comprehensive report on the vast and complicated Soviet health and medical care program. It is rather a report of impressions gained from interviews with various officials of the All-Union Ministry of Health, officials of various institutions and agencies in the health field, and visits to medical and health facilities in Moscow, Leningrad and Kiev.

The officials of the Soviet Union are proud of their hospitals, polyclinics, and health resorts, and eager to have us visit them. They were, it is true, somewhat reluctant to grant our request to visit institutions for the aged, which we finally did see; and they were unwilling to let us visit institutions or services for delinquents, or for the seriously ill, whether mentally, physically, or chronically ill.

As far as we know, the Soviet Union has the most extensively organized system of public medical care services in the world. According to expert British observers, it is more comprehensive than even the British system. There is no part of the vast Soviet domain, from Siberia to Mongolia to the Black Sea, that, by legal design, does not have its polyclinics, hospitals, rest homes, doctors, *feldshers* and district nurses. According to the central medical care plan, every family regardless of where it lives is entitled to similar medical services and similar protection of health.

It is impossible to go very far in comparisons between the medical care program of the Soviet Union and that of Great Britain or the United States because there are no uniform medical statistics in the Soviet Union, nor has there been any report of any comprehensive study by independent experts.

Observers interested in the field have had to content themselves with reporting what they saw in a relatively few hospitals, polyclinics, and health facilities in a limited number of communities.

The Soviet free medical care program provides for every aspect of medical care and health protection: case-finding, direct patient care, prevention of illness, health education, sanitation, industrial hygiene, rest and convalescence—in short, the entire range of services considered necessary for health maintenance according to modern standards.

Certain segments of the program—for example, prenatal care and health supervision of infants and young children—appear to have been most meticulously developed, especially in the large cities, through the extraordinarily well-organized system of district doctors and patronage sisters (visiting nurses) who are required to make regular home visits. The highly developed school health examination program, extending throughout the Soviet Union, is another important means of supervising the health of children and the care being given them by their parents. Summer camps are an added adjunct; very few children are seen in the large cities in August.

Polyclinic services are readily accessible to all adults, and there are special polyclinics for children. The polyclinics take the place of the traditional family doctor and some patients with whom we spoke expressed explicitly their friendly feelings toward them. How satisfactory the polyclinic is in meeting the medical needs is difficult to say. The fact that some private medical practice still goes on in the Soviet Union may or may not be one small clue.

Figures on the volume of services provided by polyclinics, hospitals, and other medical facilities were not available.

In pre-revolutionary Russia, health services had been a part of a broad community service organization called the *zemstvo*, established in 1864. The *zemstvo* formed the basis of the medical organization now administered by the Soviet government.

Dr. Sigerist, in his report on Soviet medicine,* pointed out that ". . . Soviet medicine was not created from air; there were foundations to build upon. There was scientific tradition in Russian medicine . . . There were universities training good physicians. There was medical organization giving service to the rural population."

The uniform and highly centralized pattern of organization for health and medical services is centered in the All-Union Ministry of Health in Moscow. There is also a Ministry of Health in each of the individual republics, which directs and controls all preventive, diagnostic and curative health work, as well as medical education and research within the republic. Within each republic there are also district organizations on regional and local levels.

Every Soviet enterprise has a trade union factory committee and a Communist party committee, each with a series of subcommittees that deal, among other matters, with health. These committees control hygienic conditions in the plant and in the nurseries and kindergartens maintained for the children of workers in the plant. They also have authority in deciding on which workers are to be sent to rest homes and health resorts.

Hospitals and sanatoria maintained under local budgets are supervised by their local soviets, which are also responsible for appointing guardians for insane persons, organizing sanitary inspections, combating venereal disease, and developing physical culture programs.

---

* Ibid., p. 121.

The very important Central Executive Committee of the Communist party has its own Committee on Public Health. While the Committee has no administrative function, its influence in the health field must be acknowledged.

"Its task is to watch developments, study conditions and issue policies. It obviously has a great influence. There is no doubt that in the public health field Lenin's principle, 'centralized direction and decentralized activity,' has been fully realized," says Dr. Sigerist.

Health and welfare measures depend on the active participation of various local committees for implementation. Committees in the apartment houses and those attached to factories, schools and trade unions have direct obligations in connection with sanitation, utilization of medical services, industrial hygiene, health education, child health and child rearing.

Following this pattern, committee members are expected to go into the homes of their neighbors or co-workers to learn about health problems and to give advice on how to deal with these. Since some of these very committees have authority for decisions regarding allocation of housing space, approval of applications for admission to rest homes and other important welfare services, it might be expected that families receiving advice in matters pertaining to health conditions would be influenced.

It is difficult, if not impossible, to know what health conditions actually obtain in a local community, republic or the entire Soviet Union, since none of the indices upon which it is usual to base such an assessment are available.

Maternal and child mortality in the Soviet Union, very high in the past, seem to have been very much reduced. Because of lack of statistical information it is difficult, however, to measure the changes that are reported to have occurred in maternal or child mortality, or in the incidence of rickets, malaria and other diseases.

Again and again it was our experience—and the experience of most professional observers—to ask factual questions about various aspects of medical and health services in the local community only to be told that statistics were not available. When inquiry was made at the office of the republic or at the All-Union Ministry, we were told that the figures were available only at the local level.

A striking feature of the Soviet medical and health organization is the apparently plentiful supply of doctors, nurses and other medical personnel. We were told that there are over 300,000 doctors and surgeons, approximately one for each 720 persons. In the United States we have 229,000, approximately one doctor for each 750 persons. Equally significant is the development of auxiliary medical workers such as 800,000 *feldshers,* nurses and other assisting medical workers.

The eighty-one medical institutes (separate from universities) and the 650 "middle" medical schools in the Soviet Union are steadily producing doctors and other medical personnel in the great numbers the government believes are needed.

Physicians in the Soviet Union receive their medical training in medical institutes located throughout the country. All the institutes combined are said to graduate 23,000 to 25,000 doctors annually.

In one of these institutes, the Second Medical Institute of Moscow, it was reported that there are 4,000 students, with about 600 graduating annually, of whom 60 per cent are women. Here there are said to be ten applications for each vacancy, with half the students coming from Moscow and its environs. A prominent authority in the field of medical education, who visited the Soviet Union in the spring of 1956 as a member of a medical mission from England, expressed disappointment in not being able to verify information regarding medical education in the Soviet Union.*

As to the medical students, they look young, much younger than medical students in the United States. They begin their

* C. F. Brockington, Professor of Social and Preventive Medicine, University of Manchester, "Medical Education in the USSR." *The Journal of the Society of Medical Officers of Health,* 1956.

medical training generally at seventeen or eighteen, after approximately ten years of previous schooling—which explains why they are younger.

Most medical institutes have three main fields of specialization: medicine and surgery; pediatrics; and public health.

A careful review of the Soviet medical training program by a qualified study group concluded that the training is less extensive than American training in those areas which coincide with premedical training here, that is, the general sciences, chemistry, biochemistry and biology. "Our program of medical instruction in clinical subjects is probably based on more modern methods and is perhaps somewhat more extensive especially if the internship requirement is considered, a requirement which does not exist in Soviet medical education. Medical practice in Soviet programs lasts only about sixteen weeks during the entire six years of training, and is certainly quite inadequate for a physician's training . . . As far as range in coverage in special medical subjects is concerned, perhaps the training of the two countries is comparable, but in view of all the other reservations, the Soviet professional certificate as a physician (*vrach*) appears to be somewhat below our M.D. degree."*

Several observers, in particular the members of the medical mission from England who visited in 1956, report their belief that the final product of Soviet medical education is a "technical expert" rather than a "professional with wisdom." Another observer, Dr. John D. Kershaw, in the *Public Health Journal,* April 1956, notes that the physicians are not "members of a professional class, but rather technicians on a basis comparable with engineers, scientific workers and skilled mechanics."

The salaries earned by physicians in the Soviet Union are a further indication of the position of the physician in the occupational scale. A district medical officer, for example, earns a salary in the same range as any other technician, that is, from 800 to as much as 5,000 rubles a month. The district medical

* *Soviet Professional Manpower.*

officer may earn a salary at the lower end of the range, while the director of a medical institution will be at the upper end. A taxi driver may earn 1,200 rubles a month, or 50 per cent more than the district medical officer. Still, while the income of doctors in comparison with other technicians and taxi drivers is not too favorable, there is prestige attached to being a doctor, and applications for medical school training, as we have already mentioned, are far in excess of openings.

The large proportion of women physicians and women medical students is striking. One observer reported that in a maternity hospital, seventy of the seventy-five doctors were women. Of the physicians we met while in the Soviet Union, at least three-fourths were women; a few women held high positions.

Even before the emergence of the Soviet regime, emphasis in Russia had been given to the training of "middle" medical personnel. While physicians, general practitioners and specialists, pediatricians, hygienists, dentists and pharmacists are educated in institutes of university standing and constitute the higher medical personnel, the "middle" medical personnel —*feldshers*, midwives, medical nurses, nursery nurses, patronage nurses and laboratory technicians—are educated in secondary medical schools.

The *feldsher* (and his female counterpart, the *feldsheritsa*) is peculiarly a Russian institution. Before the revolution, the special functions of the *feldsher* were to assist the physicians, carry out their instructions, practice minor surgery, vaccinate and assist in fighting epidemics. During the pre-Soviet era, many rural medical stations, because of the shortage of physicians, were headed only by *feldshers*.

After 1917 there was a tendency to discontinue this professional category. Soon, however, it became apparent that the country needed *feldshers*, especially in the rural districts, where there was an inadequate number of physicians. From 1929 on, the training of *feldshers* was stepped up. By 1944 some 460,000 *feldshers* were reported in the Soviet Union. Sigerist comments that "there is undoubtedly some degree of danger in letting half-trained doctors practice medicine . . . In practice, however, it is infinitely better to have half-trained doctors in certain rural districts than no doctors at all. The Russian 'feldsher' can be compared to the American public health nursing program in the country, with the difference that the 'feldsher' is also trained in minor surgery and obstetrics."

The *feldsher's* training in the secondary medical school includes some 4,500 instruction hours devoted to practice, laboratory work and classroom instruction.

Nursing had no tradition in old Russia. Before the revolution there had been no nursing profession in the modern sense. Instead there were sisters of mercy, members of semi-religious orders, who had little formal preparation for nursing. Regular schools of nursing connected with hospitals were established some time after the revolution, when, with the development of many new medical institutions and nurseries under the Soviet regime, the need for trained nurses was great.

The course of training for nurses has been two years following graduation from a seven-year school. Training for specialized functions, like those performed by the patronage nurses who carry social and welfare responsibilities, seems to consist of apprenticeship training under the close supervision of doctors and psychiatrists.

Medical nurses are nurses who work in hospitals, polyclinics, factory infirmaries, and other types of medical care programs where medicine and surgery are practiced.

The *nursery nurse* is a person who has had nursing training and then practices in the field of infant and child care, working under supervision of educators in day and night nurseries, boarding schools and camps.

The *patronage nurse* performs some functions similar to the health visitor in England and others like the public health nurse in America in helping carry out medical and health care services; she works in close collaboration with the district physician. Each doctor in a medical district is supposed to have available to him two patronage nurses to carry out the home-visiting program for infants under one year.

The home-visiting program is the cornerstone in provision of medical care and the basis of many aspects of the child's future health regimen and education. Each infant, during the first month of his life, is visited at home by the doctor and patronage nurse, the latter required to make not less than two visits during this period. During the rest of the first year, the patronage nurse is expected to visit each child in her district at least once a month.

The responsibilities of the doctor and nurse in these home visits have been spelled out in an article, "Patronage of All Healthy Children Under One Year," published in a Soviet medical journal. "The doctor and nurse not only have the right but are duty-bound, as representatives of a governmental agency, to demand from the mother an adequate child-rearing. Both parents in equal degree carry responsibilities for non-assumption of parental duties . . . Each doctor and nurse must know well all the children living in the district assigned to them. This includes all the social-environmental facts regarding each family group."*

Special attention is given to children under three years of age, especially newborn and babies under a year. This means knowing not only their medical and health picture, but all the important facts affecting each family group, and its ability to follow suggestions on the care of the children. Parents are expected to follow carefully the health supervision plan set for them by the district doctors and patronage sisters. These home visits by the doctor and patronage sister are correlated with the medical supervision given at the children's polyclinic to the babies and young children.

Each maternity home has its own specially appointed pa-

* *Journal Pediatria,* No. 5, 1941.

tronage nurse, who has the responsibility for transmitting the names of newborn infants to the district patronage sisters; home visits to the mother and newborn baby begin as soon as the mother returns home from the hospital.

In 1941, the patronage nurse system was extended so that prophylactic patronage of all healthy children under one year would be included in the health program. With the establishment of this principle, the number of patronage nurses was increased so that at least two patronage nurses would be available to each doctor in a medical district. As mentioned earlier, the duties of the doctor and nurse in carrying out the system of patronage include observation, surveillance and active provision of help to mothers and children that may last months and sometimes years. They are cautioned against "the serious gaps, crude mistakes and old passive methods of work that hampered this service in the past," and are reminded that "environmental help must be entwined with purely legal help; medical support takes turns with educational measures."

It is especially in the work with unwed mothers that social patronage, as distinct from medical active patronage, is carried on. The difference in these two types of work is mainly in the extension of environmental and legal aid given.

Considerable attention in working with unwed mothers must be given by the social patronage worker to such legal problems as establishment of paternity, meeting requirements of support orders, and other forms of help. Single pregnant women, those pregnant out of wedlock, divorced or deserted during pregnancy, are identified as early as possible. The groups considered to be in need of particular consideration are pregnant minors, those from out of town without established residence, houseworkers, and those living in bad housing. The need is stressed to grant legal and moral assistance as a means of combating abortion, desertion of babies, and abandonment of foundlings.

Help given to one unwed mother through social patronage is described in the article. The neighbors informed the Children's Consultation that this mother treated her nursing baby badly and was not spending properly the financial allowance she was receiving. A home visit by the patronage nurse and a committee of volunteers brought to light the fact that the baby was not fed on time and was kept in unsanitary condition, and that the mother neglected to bring the child to the polyclinic as advised. She was considered to be under the bad influence of the baby's father; she was not working and was leading a "flighty life."

Through the patronage nurse, the committee and other governmental agencies, a number of steps were taken to improve the condition of the child. The baby was placed in an institution, the mother was placed in a job, and the action of the father was reported to the administrative committee of his factory.

The mother was visited regularly by the committee, and was required to report to the Social Rights Department, which administers the special program for unwed mothers. This department continued its supervision in this case of the mother, even though the baby had already been placed in a creche.

It would appear that medical service is available and organized in such a way that patients are able to obtain care fairly rapidly. At least this seemed true in the facilities we visited and as reported by others. Certainly we never saw lines in front of any medical facilities as we did in front of food stores, or as we see lines waiting in some crowded clinics in our country.

Since the doctor, under the Soviet system, is employed by the state to give medical services according to the needs of those who call upon him in hospital and polyclinic, or summon him for home visits, he must meet these requests promptly and efficiently; delay and inefficiency are deemed neglect of duty and are legally subject to punishment. Hazard refers to two cases of public health doctors who were indicted for neglect in care of patients.*

---

* John N. Hazard, *Law and Social Change in the U.S.S.R.*, pp. 116, 118.

The Soviet doctor's freedom of choice as to the type of facility in which he will practice appears to be severely limited. If his specialty is surgery, which requires a hospital facility, he does not have the choice that the American or British physician has in respect to the type of hospital in which he will practice.

That the doctor is considered a technician may have implications in the doctor-patient relationship as we are accustomed to regard it, and tends to release him from the aura of the traditional "man of wisdom." On the basis of many conversations with our guides and other Russians about their own medical care experiences and from our observation of patients in hospitals and polyclinics, it is our impression that relations between doctors and patients are generally friendly and that patients take for granted their right to medical service.

Gifts by parents to doctors, a very common practice the world over, can take on an entirely different meaning in this society. Hazard, for example, refers to the case of a doctor who was charged with bribery—a serious offense in the Soviet Union—because he accepted gifts of farm products from the relatives of a patient in his hospital.

The existence of private practice, a subject difficult to pin down, brought varying answers to our queries. From official sources we understood that private practice does not exist in the Soviet Union. Individuals told us again and again that there is private practice. Some professional people, doctors and dentists with whom we and friends talked unofficially, told us private practice is an important source of added income for doctors and dentists. The range of services which a doctor may carry in private practice excludes surgery or any other treatment requiring hospital equipment. One American doctor with whom we visited some facilities told us of lengthy discussions he had had with a Soviet doctor about his own private practice. An English doctor, in a book on medicine in the Soviet Union, also referred to the existence of private practice.

Information on the subject is fragmentary, and we can do no more than indicate that some private medical practice apparently does exist and is permitted or at least winked at. Apparently some Soviet citizens do, for whatever reasons, pay out of their own funds for medical care.

Soviet hospitals, which provide general and specialized care in medicine and surgery, are inpatient institutions and have no outpatient services as are general in the United States and Great Britain. Neuropsychiatric hospitals are a specialized facility, not part of the general hospitals, usually large inpatient institutions caring for both children and adults; they sometimes have ambulatory services.

The polyclinics are large general outpatient centers which combine the functions of a hospital outpatient department with those of a family doctor. Patients may expect continuous attendance here except for emergencies, which are met by special emergency squads. Patients may telephone to make appointments.

People living in the neighborhood of a polyclinic look upon it as their own health resource. The polyclinic staff includes physicians who are clinical specialists in many fields. All polyclinics follow a similar pattern.

One of these polyclinics we visited in Moscow served a population of some 70,000. It was housed in a good modern building; the rooms were comfortable and not crowded. The staff included eight doctors and eleven dentists.

In a report describing one polyclinic, a British expert (Dr. Kershaw) states that a comparison of the working conditions of the Soviet district medical officer shows that this medical officer does not carry as heavy a load as the busy general practitioner in Great Britain.

For children, there are special polyclinics and child health services are reported to be similar to those in the Western countries. Infant welfare clinics are also similar to those in the United States, but attendance seems to be more regular.

It is considered "good form" to take infants and preschool children regularly to the children's polyclinics; actually, as we know from our observation and from official reports, this is a requirement. If infants and children are not brought to clinics as expected, the patronage nurse visits the home and if this is not effective, members of the various committees in the apartment house or at the factory will bring pressure upon the parents to conform. Emphasis is also given to school health work, and a comprehensive program of complete annual medical inspections is carried on for all children.

There are specialized "dispensaries" offering services in the field of neuropsychiatry. These are districted outpatient facilities and are related, on the one hand, to the polyclinics and on the other to the specialized neuropsychiatric institutes.

One substantial difference in the character of medical service between the Soviet Union and our country grows out of the Soviet housing problem, which makes it practically impossible at this time to care for seriously ill persons in their homes. Because of the extreme housing shortage in large cities, a good deal of the care given at home in the United States and in England must, perforce, be given in hospitals.

The well-known health resorts and rest homes of the Soviet Union are an important feature of the Soviet medical and health program. These are located mainly in the south, near the sea, or in the mountains. Frequently they are set up for the children or adults of the families of workers in a given industry. For example, a tuberculosis sanatorium for the children of railway workers is located in Tashkent, and children from the ages of four to seventeen are sent there from all parts of the Soviet Union, some of them thousands of miles from home.

We ourselves could not travel to see these resorts, but we talked with trained observers who had seen them, and read reports about them. They seem to be large institutions, emphasizing an institutional approach to the care of sick children and adults more popular in the United States at the turn of the century than our present more "individualized" approach.

Factory medical services are an important feature of the Soviet medical care program. We had no opportunity to observe any facility of this type. Nor did we see any institution specializing in the care of chronically ill persons or those caring for the hopelessly insane. This omission was not from choice but the result of selections made for us by the authorities.

Our opportunities for visiting medical facilities were limited, as apparently are those of other observers in this field. In general, foreign observation seems to be limited to four communities—Moscow, Leningrad, Kiev and Tashkent. In the summer of 1957, a group of American doctors did visit several additional places.

Practically every report on health and medical care in the Soviet Union has raised the question: were the places we were shown the "show places" or were they a representative selection of the good, the bad and the in-between? Most observers have felt that they were shown the best, a common practice in most countries. We believe that we saw a little of each among those we visited, and that our visit to the hospital in Leningrad was, by fortunate circumstance, an opportunity to see one large facility that was not at all a "show place."

In the main, the hospitals we did visit were in old buildings but clean and well-kept. Wards were more crowded than we have come to regard as desirable, but not more crowded than some hospitals in large cities in the United States. Equipment was adequate, with emphasis on utility rather than aesthetics. Personnel was more than plentiful. In the three large cities where we saw hospitals, we were told there were plenty of doctors and nurses and, indeed, this seemed evident everywhere.

Moreover, patients seemed always to be at ease with the doctors.

The visit to a maternity hospital in Moscow was made more meaningful because the guide-interpreter who accompanied me was the mother of two young children who had been born in this hospital. Earlier, she had had an abortion here. Her genuine enthusiasm and warm attitude toward the institution and her confidence in the doctors and quality of care she received could not but influence my own opinion.

The Krupskaya Hospital (Maternity Hospital No. 6) is named for Lenin's widow. It is one of thirty-six maternity hospitals in Moscow, a city of six million population. Any resident of Moscow may choose to go to whichever of these hospitals she prefers. This freedom of choice is somewhat surprising in relation to the very close and intensive system of follow-up exercised by the patronage nurses in relation to infants.

At Krupskaya Hospital the chief doctor is a woman. At the time of my visit her assistant, a man, was head of the medical division. The chief doctor herself was the warm, serious, dedicated type of person we were growing accustomed to meet in these health services.

When I came into her office, it was apparent that something unusual was going on. There was a flurry of cameras and spotlights, and I saw a young American newspaperman talking excitedly through and with his interpreter about his wish to photograph an abortion procedure. The Russian abortion law had been changed less than a year before and he was trying to convince the hospital officials that Americans would be interested in learning about techniques of abortion legally sanctioned. The usual difficulties of communication seemed to be weighing down doctors, Intourist guide and American newspaperman. The young American suggested that we join in their discussion. We tried this for a few minutes, but things became even more confusing. I explained that my primary interest was in learning about maternal and infant care, although I would like to know about the new program. The chief doctor decided to guide us through the hospital and stayed with us during the entire visit.

The hospital has approximately 4,500 babies born there each year. A full-time staff of forty-three doctors, one hundred and thirty sisters (nurses or midwives) and eighty attendants carry out the program.

The doctors who give prenatal care are not the doctors who will deliver the babies. The confidence of the patient seems to be in the institution rather than in an individual obstetrician. This impression came from many sources.

Of its 200 beds, thirty are reserved for patients with pathological problems of pregnancy. These are usually complications of pregnancy such as hypertension or infection. In answer to my inquiries I learned that about 3 per cent of the patients who give birth here come to the hospital during some part of their prenatal period. The length of stay of approximately 99 per cent of the patients is eight to ten days following delivery; about one per cent remain longer.

Interest in premature babies, a subject of growing concern in the United States, prompted me to ask in detail about their care. The mother of a premature baby remains in the hospital for two weeks. If at the end of that time the baby is still too small to go home, he is sent to a special institution for premature babies.

I inquired about the volume of legal abortions in the hospital and was told that since November 1955, when the new law permitting legal abortion went into effect, the hospital has performed fifteen to twenty abortions a week. The staff seemed matter-of-fact about their work in this field. They encouraged us to visit the wards of patients who were either awaiting abortion or convalescing from the procedure. In the main, these women were in their thirties or forties, with only a few in the younger age group. As in other rooms and wards, the patients in this group were lying in bed, reading or doing nothing. The atmosphere was serene. I could not tell if this was usual or because of an official visit.

In answer to our questions, the doctors said the government action regarding legalization of abortion was taken to protect women from unnecessary infection. We understood that doctors and patronage nurses have preliminary discussion with the patients before the decision is made to have an abortion.

Our tour took in every part of the hospital, including all delivery rooms, babies' nurseries and operating rooms.

The atmosphere of the hospital was cheerful, with a clean, starched look, and an orderliness balanced by comfort. The patients seemed well cared for and the procedures were humane and considerate. The standard of care would compare favorably with that in good hospitals in any part of the world. There were some differences in the rooms; some patients were in wards with seven or eight beds, others in rooms like our private or semi-private rooms. Beds were generally closer together. Equipment was fairly modern and in good condition, and supplies were plentiful.

We saw women in labor and we saw women in the delivery rooms. Midwives and attendants were always near them; the patients seemed never to be alone in any room. In each delivery room there were at least two patients, and in the labor rooms there were five or six. The atmosphere was quiet and controlled. I do not recall hearing any cries or moans or seeing any woman in the panicky state one sometimes encounters in our hospitals.

Midwives were hovering over patients in labor and talking to them. I could see from the heavy perspiration on their faces that the women in the labor rooms were suffering, but they did not moan. The delivery tables were plain white metal and not equipped with stirrups.

What was most striking about this experience was the extraordinary self-control of the patients, which was apparently taken for granted by the staff. I could not help but think of the quietness of the two-year-olds awakening without a murmur or movement in the nurseries in Kiev. What is the meaning of such self-control seen in two-year-olds and in mothers in labor? We have no answer but we know it is drastically different from anything in the United States. The physical closeness of the midwives to the women in labor, their patience and the relaxed pace of the entire procedure seemed to contribute to the atmosphere of assurance.

Judging from the average length of stay of eight to ten

days, which is longer than in our maternity hospitals, many more patients were in bed than would be the case in a maternity hospital in our country. It was my impression that the tempo of convalescence following delivery is slower and more like the tempo we practiced a decade ago.

Mothers are encouraged to breast-feed their babies for the first few months. As far as possible, human milk is used for all babies at least for a few months. I saw many mothers having their breasts pumped to provide breast milk for infants whose own mothers were not producing milk. In the large cities, I was told there are many stations where breast milk is available for feeding of infants.

Infants in the nurseries were lying in clean, neat bassinets, closely arranged, touching one another. The infants were wrapped tightly, arms and feet inside, in blankets with one end of the blanket covering the head. They were propped up on a slanting surface.

Premature babies were in the same nursery, not in incubators such as we are accustomed to use in caring for them. Premature babies, those under three pounds, were lying in the common type of bassinet with two or three hot-water bags surrounding them and with no other equipment.

"How do you deal with infections in infants and mothers?" I asked Dr. M. "We do not have infections," she answered.

It did not seem possible to me that in as active a hospital as this no infections whatever would occur. I thought she might not have understood my question. I pointed out that in our best hospitals infections, such as dysentery in infants or colds, occur from time to time. I asked if she could explain how they avoid these rather common difficulties. She picked up a gauze mask which visitors and hospital personnel are required to wear whenever they enter a nursery or operating room, and said: "This is how we avoid infections." I said that this was a usual practice in our hospitals, too, but that it did not seem sufficient to eliminate infections.

Later in the tour of the hospital Dr. M. pointed out a special nursery. She said it was used to isolate infants who might develop infection, and added she was showing me this to help me understand that there were no cases of infection and that this nursery was being used for well babies because the other nurseries were crowded.

On the way back from the tour of the building I again brought up with the two head doctors my lingering question about the problem of infections. The doctors realized I was still puzzled by their answer and one of them, in an effort to help me understand, said that perhaps there were other factors that might be contributing to their great success in avoiding infections. They said that in maternity hospitals they have a firm policy prohibiting any outside visitors. No father, regardless of his position or occupation, is permitted to visit his wife while she is in the hospital. As we were leaving the building we met a doctor inquiring about his wife and baby; like other fathers, he was receiving his information in the lobby.

In retrospect I have thought again and again about the tempo of the labor and delivery process. The unhurried attitude of the staff, who have no other duties during these hours than to stay with these mothers in labor, must give them a sense of comfort and security.

Considering the characteristic Soviet caution in these matters, we may assume the Krupskaya Maternity Hospital in Moscow represents one of the finest maternity facilities in the Soviet Union. This was a hospital which Intourist authorities were not only willing to permit Americans to visit but where they permitted visitors to photograph what they saw. It was not possible to assess how the patients felt about the care they were receiving. In general, they seemed relaxed.

We learned from another observer, an American visiting industrial plants, that on his visits to factories he had seen two delivery chairs in the infirmary of a shoe factory in Leningrad.

On a visit to a famous collective farm (named for Lenin) about thirty miles outside Moscow, I asked to see the infirmary and particularly the facilities for maternity and infant care. We were given permission to go to the nursery for young children. The request to see the infirmary, however, was met with the answer: "The infirmary is closed for repairs." I said I could understand if the place was in some disorder because of repairs, but that I would appreciate seeing what type of building and facilities were included in a collective. I asked if I could have special permission to go with one of the guides to see what the building looked like from the outside. This request was denied.

In our interview with the staff of the Ministry of Social Security we indicated we were particularly interested in knowing about the care of older people—especially those in homes for the aged. There are some 500 homes for the aged in the Soviet Union. Most of these have a bed capacity of 100 to 2,500; several have only fifty beds.

Admission to homes for the aged is based on the desire of the older person to go into a home. In general, admission for women is at fifty-five and for men at sixty. The Ministry of Social Security believes older people should be sent to homes in their own region. The local social security administration is the source through which arrangements are made for admission. Care is free of charge. Those who are on invalid pensions receive from 10 to 25 per cent of their pensions; the remainder goes to the family. In some homes where there is work occupation, the resident receives 50 per cent of the money he earns, the other 50 per cent going to the home.

Because of discussion of this topic in our country, we tried to find out how the staff of the Ministry felt about institutional care for older people. We asked if there is a view that older people should go to homes for the aged or remain in their own homes. They indicated that this is not controversial, but that homes are open to all who are eligible and that it is in general "more sensible" for the aged people to go to homes.

The next afternoon the Deputy Minister of Social Security, who has responsibility for all the programs for the aged, including social insurance and institutional care, accompanied us to visit a home for the aged sixty or seventy miles outside of Moscow.

The home is in a small country town far from any center of

population amid a beautiful countryside. As I traveled further and further into the rural area approaching the home, I found we were driving from one dirt road to another even more primitive. I wondered about accessibility to this home during the long winter months when snow and ice would make these roads practically impassable.

The home itself is set about a mile away from the nearest tiny village where we saw a cluster of perhaps a dozen small houses. Beautiful woods were all about the area and orchards surrounded the home itself. The main building is of brick, three stories high, designed very much like many of the older type we still see in the United States or England.

Before we went through the building we stopped for a preliminary conference in the office of the director, much as we had done on visits to other institutions. The director had with him his assistant administrator, the woman doctor in charge of patients' medical care, and the chairman of the residents' soviet (council). As is the custom, the director asked me to list my questions and to indicate what I wished to see in the home.

"I am eager to learn how you keep your residents happy and satisfied," I said. "In our country, for example, we sometimes have difficulty in providing sufficiently interesting menus."

The director laughed and said this was no problem to them because the residents decide for themselves what their menus are to be. From this beginning we talked about how the home is managed and the kind of responsibility the administration gives to residents. They told me about their residents' council, which consists of fifteen elected members who have the major responsibility for outlining service tasks to be done and to decide on many aspects of the program within the institution. These responsibilities include planning of menus; recreation; "labor therapy"; and many other activities. The members of the council are elected by the full meeting of residents. Once in three months, at the full meeting, reports are given on all these responsibilities.

The number of residents is 300, 209 women and 91 men.

The age range of the older residents is from fifty-five to one hundred. There are five who are ninety-five years of age. I visited one of these who was in bed. There were in addition two young people of eighteen who are chronically ill and, for reasons I could not ascertain, are residents of the home.

The staff consists of a director, an assistant director, two doctors, five senior nursing sisters and twenty-eight younger educational sisters.

Residents are expected to get up at seven-thirty A.M. and have their breakfast at eight-thirty. By half-past nine they are ready to walk or go to "labor therapy." I had a little difficulty understanding at first what this meant. It seemed to mean household and work tasks around the home that were assigned by the council.

Other activities that some residents engaged in were laboratory, library, radio or reading room work. Dinner is served at one o'clock and residents are expected to rest for an hour after that. At seven-thirty in the evening supper is served, and at eleven o'clock residents are expected to go to bed.

Recreational activities seem to center around listening to radios and watching television. There are seven television sets and five radios. Sometimes there are dramas which they themselves enact, or they may watch movies. The staff told us with much enthusiasm that occasionally they have lectures, but what excited the residents most were occasional outings such as a trip to see the great Agricultural Exposition in Moscow. Visitors from a distance were a rarity, judging by the excitement our visit occasioned.

The young woman doctor told us about her medical program. From nine to eleven every morning she visits in the rooms of the residents and examines in their beds any residents who do not feel well. From eleven to one she has office hours in her study and sees any residents who come to her with physical complaints. She has sufficient equipment, she said, to take care of the usual minor medical needs of older people. If they are ill and require more extensive care, they are sent away to a hospital.

Our tour through the home was a rather startling experience and I had from the beginning the feeling that this was a real occasion. The fact that the All-Union Deputy Minister was visiting was in itself probably most important. Added to that, few of the residents had ever met an American, and thus I was a subject of considerable interest.

Among the residents was a woman in her sixties who had lost the sight of one eye in the last war as a fighter in the Red Army. She was still a vigorous, aggressive woman and she followed me, alternately begging and ranting for peace, *mir*, with Russia. I had the feeling that the administrator did not try to divert her since she stayed with us wherever we went during my entire visit. The assumption in her comments was that "peace" is Russia's wish and that the threat of war comes from America.

We went from room to room, and I realized, after a time, that because the event was so important we were going to have to go into practically all the dormitories. The feelings of the residents were too sensitive to allow me to skip a room. Most rooms, especially those of the women, had stiffly starched white counterpanes heavily embroidered with intricate lace trimmings. Many beds had three or four huge pillows with white ruffles of handmade lace.

One room, a very special one in location and furnishings, was the home of three unusual and special people. One was a former celebrated ballet dancer. She had a huge picture of herself in tights on the wall, together with two handsome Japanese hangings. She shared the room with a former teacher and a former principal of a school. This room was without a doubt the most attractive in the home.

The spirit of the home seemed vital and very good. There was no apparent program for occupational therapy, no activity program in our sense. I wondered if the frequent expressions of gratitude given to the officials by the residents for their comforts were genuine and spontaneous, or were made because they felt obligated to do so.

The rooms in the institution varied in size. Some had as few as three or four beds, most had eight or nine. A few large rooms had twelve and fifteen beds. Most of the residents had brought a few treasures of their own—pictures of family members and examples of their own handwork.

I was puzzled by the fact that in a home for the aged I saw so few religious objects or expressions of religious interest. One elderly woman clutched me as I came down the hall toward her door and led me to her window to show off an ikon which she had hanging in a recessed part of the window-frame. I realized that the authorities knew she had the ikon when they smiled indulgently. This was the only evidence of religious interest that I saw. I did notice, as we walked outside of the building, a church across a field from the home. I asked about the church and the comment was, "We do not prohibit people from going to the services." I was not invited to see the church and therefore do not know if it was a "functioning" church. My impression was that it was not.

As a whole, the institution seemed orderly and well organized. The rooms were clean. By our standards, however, the kitchens seemed hardly sanitary. In fact, the flies and the garbage and the smells in the small rooms where the food was prepared made it difficult, almost impossible, for me to eat with relish the lavish tea-supper that was prepared with such friendliness and eagerness. The meal consisted of herring, ham, other cold meats, cheese, several kinds of salad, pumpernickel bread, and freshly baked coffee cake. This was obviously a special spread, and I noticed the pleasure with which it was eaten by several of the resident staff.

Because the chairman of the residents' council impressed me as an able administrative person and seemed to be carrying a good deal of direct administrative responsibility, I asked about his background. I was told that he was a former *feldsher* and had worked for twenty years as an occupational therapist in the Kashenka Hospital, the outstanding psychiatric hospital and research center in Moscow which we have described earlier.

At tea, I asked about a matter that puzzled us.

As we had gone through the home I had seen no bed-bound residents. The one ninety-five-year-old patient was merely resting in bed. Considering the number of people living here and their age range, this seemed an unusual situation and one which would not be found in a comparable home for the aged in the United States or England. I asked the administrator and doctor what happens to residents who do not feel well, who have a short-term illness or who have chronic illness. They said this was no problem in their home. If a resident becomes ill, he is transferred to another institution for sick elderly people. In answer to further questions about illness, they said they had no infirmary in this home. They said that there was a hospital not too far away. This home, they made clear, was a residence for well people.

I visited a general hospital in Leningrad with two American doctors, one a surgeon and the other an anesthetist. The latter was to be in the Soviet Union a very short time and this was to be her major visit to a hospital. She had spent months making the arrangements for this opportunity and had written many letters from the United States to get permission. Like many of the other visits foreigners made to professional places, this one had a long history of difficulties. In spite of previous arrangements that had been agreed to by Intourist, it took the doctor hours of persistent inquiry, telephoning, confirmation and reconfirmation to bring about the actual visit.

We were sorry to see her have so much trouble but relieved to find that such difficulties happened to others besides ourselves. I came upon her in the lobby of our hotel when she had just received permission, and I was delighted when she generously offered to include me in this trip.

The hospital we were taken to visit was an old building like many others we had seen, but the poverty of the equipment and the general bareness of furnishings made it clear that this was not one of the special hospitals often visited by foreigners.

We were received by a group in the administrator's office. The administrator was a male physician. There was also a nurse in charge who had a great deal of authority in the situation, and a doctor wearing army boots and an army uniform under his white coat. He was so quiet in our preliminary discussion, we thought he did not understand either German or English, the languages being used. Toward the end of the visit it was apparent he knew both languages well.

The American surgeon who accompanied us had just arrived in the Soviet Union, had read a good deal of Soviet medical literature and told the officials he knew they did the speediest surgery in the world.

We were received with graciousness and friendliness and were taken on a tour of the hospital. As we went through the wards, we had a variety of reactions. The equipment was outmoded and battered, the rooms not too clean, the beds were touching each other, fifteen or twenty in a room. Bedsteads and mattresses were dilapidated. Lack of privacy and the reliance of patients upon one another for mutual help added to the gloominess of the picture. There were spittoons near the beds and we saw bedpans and urinals under beds. One person in the group asked about bathrooms. At first the question was ignored. After he became persistent, we were told that we would see a bathroom later. Just before we left we were taken to a bathroom. It was a neglected room and the seat was off one toilet; although an effort had apparently been made to get it into order, the room was not clean and was most unattractive. We wondered if it was used.

In contrast, our visit to the laboratory showed it to be a cheerful, clean room with many growing plants and flowers all about. Girls were hard at work there. Although serious about their work, they appeared at ease.

Both the American surgeon and anesthetist were eager to see surgery. The administrator and doctors on the top staff kept explaining that an appointment for this would have to be made at another time. The Americans said they could not come again. The surgeon pressed for an opportunity to see whatever surgery was going on then and there.

"Surely," he said, "in such a big hospital, which specializes in surgery, there must be some operations now in progress."

The doctors conferred with each other and then said there was an operation going on in the surgery and that we might observe it. I, of course, had no competence to evaluate the surgery or the circumstances surrounding it. The regular anesthetist, we were told, was on vacation, and one of the nurses was administering anesthesia to the patient, who was undergoing major abdominal surgery. I noticed that the American anesthetist, after observing for a few moments, turned away and began speaking to one of the head doctors. I gathered from what I overheard that she was asking him about anesthesia. The American surgeon, too, turned away after a few moments and seemed not to want to watch the details of the operation.

When we returned to the administrator's office both the American surgeon and the American anesthetist were reluctant to discuss the surgery. The surgeon, who had been so fulsome in his praise of Soviet surgery from the literature he had been reading in America, said to the administrator, "I am sure this is not a good example of Soviet surgery. I am sure the surgeon who was operating is a student. For," he said, "the operation was being very badly done."

The anesthetist told me that she could not bear watching the way the anesthesia was being administered. She felt that the patient's life was in serious jeopardy, mainly because of the careless way in which the anesthesia was being administered. From my own observation, the surgeon who was doing the operation was hardly a student, at least in age. It was my impression that she was in her forties.

This visit, I realize, gives a radically different impression from that reported by many reliable observers whose visits were, like most of ours, carefully planned in advance and who like us often wondered whether the only places they saw were the show places of every field. This visit was completely different; no previous plan for the observation of the surgery had been arranged.

In all visits to hospitals and institutions we tried to assess the kind of relationship that exists between doctors and patients. I felt here, as I did on my visits to other medical facilities, that the patients seemed to be comfortable in their relationship to the doctors. The awed attitude we see sometimes in our country when visiting hospitals was far less evident. Doctors in Soviet Russia are treated as if taken for granted and a familiar part of daily living. Even in this hospital, lesser in quality and service than most places we visited, there was a friendly attitude between doctors and patients.

Before coming to the Soviet Union, I had been told by a professional colleague who had been in Poland in 1948 that the quality of Soviet physical rehabilitation work was extraordinarily good. In particular, I was told that the artificial limbs in use, especially aluminum appliances, were, even at that time, superior to the appliances being used in the United States now. Unfortunately, this was misleading preparation for our early observations in Moscow and later in Leningrad and Kiev, where we saw many young and middle-aged men hobbling about with stumps of legs, and many people using primitive crutches. It seemed to us that the proportion of young and middle-aged persons in need of prosthetic appliances was high, certainly higher than in many large cities in England, France, Italy and the United States.

Other observers have commented on the lack of services for the handicapped adult in the Soviet Union. Dr. Kershaw reports that "physical rehabilitation work still relies heavily on mechano-therapy as distinct from occupational therapy," and notes that not much progress has been made with rehabilitation centers as such. He says that "there has been nothing in Russia to parallel the intense and largely successful efforts in Western countries to extend the employment of the blind, particularly in the fields formerly regarded as the normal person's preserve. It is true that the scheme of sheltered workshops can work more effectively in a totalitarian state than in an individualistic one, but the new and growing independence of the disabled in Britain has a more than economic value."

This is not to say that some rehabilitation efforts are not moving forward. At the time of our visit special schools for physically handicapped children were opening in Moscow and Leningrad. The work with these and visually handicapped children is described in Chapter XIII.

XIII

Educational Programs and Resources

TO TRANSLATE national purposes into reality, a comprehensive educational program has been established for children and adults including both formal education and uses of leisure time. This example of the possibilities of planning in the field of human relations challenges the imagination by its broad outlook and many-faceted approach. What makes this even more impressive is that the program is a rapidly changing one marked by continuous expansion in scope and coverage and with constant introduction of new emphases and directions.

The unusual rate of growth of educational establishments, the increase in the number of schools and in the growth of the student body, with resultant enormous increase in literacy, represent an extraordinary achievement—one that leaves most observers breathless. This is true though even a cursory review leaves one with many questions about certain qualitative elements in the program. Our talks with Soviet educators made it clear that they too are watchful of its shortcomings.

As far back as 1908, the Imperial Russian government enacted a law which aimed to achieve compulsory school attendance for all children aged eight to eleven by 1922.

The percentage of literacy for all persons aged nine and over rose from 24 per cent in 1897 to 81.2 per cent in 1939, with most of the illiterates, as might be expected, falling into the age group of fifty and over.* While the dislocation of the war called a halt to progress, the advance has been resumed in recent years.

During the period 1933-38, 20,600 schools were built and the number of students increased from approximately 24 million to 34 million. Expenditures rose from 21 billion rubles in 1939 to 59.5 billions in 1950. This rate of expenditure has been maintained with 311.5 billion rubles spent during the fifth Five-Year Plan (1950-55).** The sixth Five-Year Plan (1956-60) provides for a building program of new town and village schools catering to four million pupils, with single-shift schooling and universal secondary education as goals.

While this report supplies figures on the increase in the number of new schools built or put into operation, as well as the number of pupils which they would serve, more information would be needed to get an accurate picture of progress in the development of this program. What seems clear, however, is that schools are being added and the number of pupils is increasing. It is also pertinent to point out that in connection with the switch-over to "universal secondary education and to single-shift schooling" that is now in progress, the sixth Five-Year Plan provides for a building program of new town and village schools catering to four million pupils.

Historically, there has been a different standard of compulsory education for children in the urban and in rural communities. It has been noted, for instance, that while the urban population in 1939 was thirty-three per cent of the total, there is a changing but still different proportion in the number of children enrolled in rural and urban areas.

There are many reasons given for this difference. One is the difference in available facilities, with the rural areas having less than the urban. Another may be the attitudes of parents toward education. A third is the economic pressure upon

---

* Michael T. Florinsky, *Towards an Understanding of the USSR.* Revised edition. New York: The Macmillan Company, 1953, p. 184.

** *Report on Public Education in the USSR for the Year 1955-56,* official publication issued in the summer of 1956.

the parents who are collective farmers which forces young boys and girls to engage in agricultural labor at an early age.*

We have referred here only to the expansion in the number of pupils and schools that is taking place. The expansion in certain specialized phases of the educational program, such as technical and higher education, will be dealt with later.

As has already been described in our discussion of child care, the Soviet educational system begins with the nursery school which accepts children from one month to three years. These are organized on a district basis or as adjuncts to factories. They consist of both residential and non-residential institutions and in the main are intended to serve children of working mothers. They are administered by the Ministry of Health.

The kindergarten, which serves children from four to seven years of age inclusive, is organized on both a municipal as well as factory basis. These are supervised by the ministries of education of the different republics and come closer in their programs to the regular day schools. There is comparatively little emphasis on academic education, on reading or writing, with most of the time devoted to music, singing, gymnastics, arts and crafts, gardening. The focus of the kindergarten program is on the development of skills and competence in speech. Parents are required to pay what they can toward the actual costs of maintaining a child in the nursery and kindergarten.

Contrary to what one might expect from the general Soviet philosophy of child rearing, as well as from the social and economic factors such as the employment of mothers and poor housing which exist in the Soviet Union at present, a comparatively small proportion of the children falling within the nursery and kindergarten age groups are enrolled within these child-care facilities. During the years 1938 and 1939, the nurseries were able to accommodate approximately 800,000 chil-

---

* *Soviet Professional Manpower.*

dren, which was something under ten per cent of all children in the pertinent age group.* By 1940, there were over 1,000,000 children enrolled in the kindergartens, or approximately nine per cent of all children in the eligible age group.

The plans call for substantial expansion of these facilities. But assuming that the target had been achieved, the total would still represent something less than twenty per cent of the children in the eligible age group.

The elementary school covers the years eight to eleven; the intermediate, twelve to fourteen; and the secondary, fourteen to seventeen.

Children attend school six days a week and the school week varies between twenty-seven and thirty-six hours. Considerable concern is presently being voiced about the burden upon the child which this represents, with pediatricians and psychiatrists urging a less burdensome schedule.

Children attend school 200 days a year, as against 180 in the United States. Taking into account the longer school week, the ten years a Russian child spends in the elementary, intermediate and secondary schools probably equals the twelve years an American child spends in elementary and high schools.

The size of classes in the kindergartens is approximately twenty-five children; in the elementary and later grades, thirty-five and forty. Because of the shortage of classrooms, most schools operate on a two-shift basis with two teachers, each on duty with his class approximately six hours. Programs projected for the years ahead envisage a gradual elimination of the two-shift arrangement.

Completion of secondary education, and actual certification to that effect, is an essential prerequisite for all types of higher education. If a student enters school at the required age of seven and goes through the regular ten-year school, he may enter a higher educational establishment at seventeen, or even younger, and graduate at the age of twenty-one or twenty-five. Sometimes immediately upon graduation from a higher

* Ibid., p. 30.

educational establishment, but more frequently after several years of experience, a student may enter advanced degree training-research lasting anywhere from three years on.*

Less fortunate or less competent pupils are diverted from regular school in the intermediate grades and channeled into outlets training skilled labor.

As an alternative to training in the upper grades of the regular secondary school, specialized secondary semi-professional training is available leading to employment at age sixteen to nineteen.

The diversion of a student to a skilled labor training program, or the termination of regular education for any other reason, does not entirely restrict his chances for further education. In various roundabout ways and even with considerable delay in years, an individual can make up his lacks.

There are a number of special schools for youth and young people which represent substitutes for attendance at the regular intermediate and secondary schools—labor youth schools, labor reserve schools and military schools.

Schools for working youth are intended for young men and women aged fourteen to twenty-five who have been forced to take employment, have been discharged from military service, or were not able for one reason or another to attend regular schools. Such schools operate in three shifts: morning, afternoon and evening, so that students may arrange their attendance according to their work schedules. Schools for rural youth operate only in the evenings.

A unique feature of the Soviet educational system is the Labor Reserve Draft. Each year since 1940, when the practice was established, as many as 400,000 young people between fourteen and seventeen have been drafted into schools of the State Labor Reserve. The first to be drafted were those who neither attended school nor were employed. The second category included over-age pupils attending the fifth to seventh

* Ibid., pp. 19-20.

grades. Another group were regular students in the intermediate grades of rural schools only.

The purpose of this draft is to channel boys into skilled labor occupations. Another purpose is to transfer young people from rural occupations into the industrial labor force. The whole concept of the labor reserve seems to contradict the repeated insistence of educational leaders that children have equal abilities.

Trade schools usually offer two to three years of training. Factory schools offer only six months to a year. Both prepare skilled labor. A third type of school, added in 1953, prepares skilled labor for agriculture.

Besides the special schools there are countless permanent or temporary apprenticeship programs.

Because our visit took place in the summer, we were not able to get any firsthand impression of the educational methods employed except as these were revealed in the preschool and kindergarten programs which we described earlier.

The impression that we gained from our talks with Russian educators was of emphasis on the traditional, formal, and what we usually refer to as Victorian methods. A firsthand glimpse of the educational practice in the elementary school is reported by a British educator who recently visited the Soviet Union.*

> In the Schools of the compulsory age range, the Victorian atmosphere of the buildings and decorations was matched by the Victorian atmosphere of the teaching. Primary education up to eleven and secondary education beyond take place in the same building, but the only real distinction between primary and secondary seems to be the qualification of the teachers. The schools are in effect full-range schools.
>
> We saw seven-year-olds taking their first reading lessons. Every child had its book open at the same page, and was pointing to the same letter with a colored pointer. When they started to write, the class sat up straight, the teacher said, "oo," the class took up their pens and made the appropriate letter, and then

---

* Peter Quince, "Russian Journey." *The Schoolmaster*, Vol. CLXX, No. 2,467, November 9, 1956, p. 642.

put their pens down again. The teacher then said, "ah," and the process was repeated. The exercise books were ruled not only horizontally, but also diagonally from top right to bottom left, so that the writing should have the same slope. A twelve-year-old painting class—it was explained that the curriculum allowed watercolor painting for the first time at that state—sat closely packed in desks with drawing boards before them, all painting a brown earthenware pot that stood on a table "out in the front." The paintings all seemed to be at the same stage of completion.

In the past a variety of schools existed whose purpose was to enable adults to make up deficiencies in their education. There were schools for adult illiterates, roughly representing the equivalent of the regular primary schools. There were also a number of programs intended to increase the vocational skills of adults, similar to the present special schools for young people. At the present time regular schools conduct evening adult education on the elementary and secondary levels.

Today those who did not attend either a regular school or a secondary semi-professional school, or their equivalent, must obtain a "maturity certificate" as proof they have completed secondary education. On rare occasions this may be done by informal training (*eksternat*), consisting simply of registration in a regular school for the purpose of taking examinations only, without required attendance or homework. Or the certificate may be obtained despite delay in years by attending various schools providing, at least in the formal sense, training equivalent to that of the regular elementary and secondary schools.*

We have before referred to the widespread participation of all people in many aspects of daily community life. Committee work in the Soviet Union can be considered an important phase of adult education.

Extension or correspondence courses are offered either by divisions of regular schools, by semi-professional schools, or by institutions set up exclusively for this particular purpose.** The illustrious Moscow University offers correspondence courses.

* *Soviet Professional Manpower,* p. 11.

** Ibid., pp. 12-14.

In the United States certain occupations are practiced by persons with college degrees. Certain others are practiced by those who have acquired skills through on-the-job experience but who have no formal training. And still others are practiced by those who have attended vocational or industrial high schools or trade schools. In the Soviet Union the *technicum* and other secondary specialized schools give formal training for persons in many of these occupations.*

The *technicum* provides teachers, nurses, shop foremen and various kinds of engineers and technicians. The number of professional skills covered can be grouped into five categories: health and medicine, engineering, education, agriculture and socio-economic fields.

While the aim of instruction in these establishments is to prepare specialists whose qualifications, skills and knowledge are sufficient for their employment on the intermediate levels of professional competence, their curricula often include the same subjects as the institutions of higher learning in the same professional fields. Very often, too, graduates of a *technicum* proceed later in life to an institute or university to secure further training and achieve full professional standing.

Until recently *technicums* accepted graduates of the Soviet seven-year intermediate schools from the age of fourteen up. With the switch to a ten-year universal education, we were told that admission to *technicums* will be largely limited to graduates of a ten-year school program. This will mean a shorter training period, heretofore four years.

The average *technicum* is a relatively small institute with about 200 students. Most *technicums* are located near industrial plants and a considerable amount of the training is carried on in the industrial establishments, with the teachers recruited or temporarily assigned from the working staff of the plant.

We found it significant that during the last twenty-five years

---

* Ibid., p. 69.

enrollment in *technicums* has increased more than fifteenfold and by 1954 was approaching 2,000,000 students.

These schools are financed, maintained and administered by the specialized ministries covering the various functions for which the schools prepare students. Thus, the Electrical Trust would probably provide training for electrical engineers and ministries responsible for agriculture would provide training for agricultural specialists. The educational ministries would provide the training for teachers. Although these *technicums* are financed and maintained by the specialized ministries, they are supervised by the Ministry of Higher Education of the Soviet Union and their curricula resemble those of the higher educational institutions in the same field.

Soviet Professional Manpower gives us a great deal of information about higher education and professional training in the Soviet Union. In the Soviet educational hierarchy the institutes and the universities fill the level above the *technicums*. In the U.S.S.R. today there are thirty-three universities and well over 800 institutes.

Universities usually offer somewhat broader training and instruction in a variety of fields, while institutes offer narrower specialization and give training primarily in related fields. While universities offer more theoretical and less applied training, institutes primarily provide applied specialized training. Although there is a present trend toward inclusion of more pure science in the training of technicians, the differentiation between the university and the institute continues.

The universities are multi-divisional training establishments and as a rule have about six faculties: (1) physical-mathematical sciences, (2) philology, (3) history, (4) geography, (5) biology and (6) chemistry. Some have many additional divisions, such as jurisprudence. Only as a rare exception is a division found in a university with such narrow applied specialization as medicine or engineering.

University training, as a rule, lasts five years. The average enrollment is about 3,000 regular students, except in Leningrad and Moscow which have almost 20,000 students each. Moscow

University has 17,000 regular and 5,000 extension students enrolled in twelve divisions and eighteen departments. Its faculty numbers 2,300, including 100 members of the Soviet Academy of Science.

Each university has its own entrance examination. The character of the applicant is taken into account in his admission. "Character" involves not only previous work experience but also a review of participation in ideological groups.

The premium placed on higher education in the U.S.S.R. is indicated by the consideration accorded young men subject to military service. If a student is already enrolled in an institution of higher education when he reaches the military draft age of eighteen, he is deferred. He may continue to be deferred until the requirements of his service are finally canceled because he continues to receive good marks and to fulfill the expectations of the educational institution.

While institutes do not give any general education, they teach enough theory to make the acquisition of applied knowledge in a given field feasible. Numerous institutes offer training in five branches of professional specialties: industrial engineering, agriculture, socio-economics, education, and health. Most of the institutes have enrollments of about 1,000 students, although a number, especially in the engineering field, have enrollments of 3,000 to 8,000. The length of training in an institute is usually four years, but may go on to six.

The two main sources for entrance to the higher educational establishments are graduation from the ten-year school or from a *technicum*. Entrants take competitive examinations; these may be dispensed with if a graduate of a secondary school has a high record of achievement.

We noted with interest that there are more applicants for admission to the universities and to some of the institutes than there are vacancies. Sometimes, as at Moscow University, the ratio is twelve applicants to one vacancy. This is partly accounted for by the fact that admission to universities and institutes located in the larger cities is highly prized, and partly by the fact that the institutes are unevenly distributed geographically. Moscow has about ninety and Leningrad about fifty higher educational establishments with a total enrollment of 280,000 in Moscow and 150,000 in Leningrad. This concentration of higher education in a few large centers is giving concern to the authorities and we learned an effort is being made to achieve a wider spread over the whole Soviet Union.

One development with special meaning for the relationship between the Western world and the Soviet Union, whether this be seen as cold war or co-existence, is the extent and training of specialists in the Soviet Union as compared with that of the Western world. An article in a British periodical,* under the title, "New Minds for the New World," reaches the conclusion that the Soviet Union is far ahead in this respect of the United States, Great Britain and the rest of the Western world.

In both the Soviet Union and the West, students at university institutions normally take their first qualifications when they are twenty-one or twenty-two years old; in the United States and Great Britain this is known as the Bachelor's degree, in Russia, the Diploma.

A comparison of all the science graduates in 1954 was as follows:

	Pure Science	Applied Science
United States	23,500 (144)	22,500 (137)
U.S.S.R.	12,000 (56)	60,000 (280)
Great Britain	5,200 (105)	2,800 (57)

The figures in parentheses express the number per million of population.

England and Russia both have a secondary supply of applied scientists. In England this has developed from the traditional apprenticeships of the early days of the Industrial Revolution and is very much tied in with apprenticeship training beginning at sixteen to eighteen—training on the job that is, with part-time formal courses at technical colleges. At twenty-one to twenty-three, they obtain the Higher National Certifi-

* *The New Statesman and Nation,* September 8, 1956.

cate from the Ministry of Education. In Russia the graduates of the *technicums* broadly represent a similar grade of technicians who usually get their training between the ages of seventeen and twenty-one. According to this article, the numbers coming out of the *technicums* are startling: 70,000 in 1954 with an estimate of at least 100,000 by 1960.

While the Russian production of pure scientists is numerically modest, Soviet Russia is now training more applied scientists per year than the United States and Western Europe put together—a fact of world significance. The Soviet Union has understood that if it is to achieve its purposes it must conquer the natural world, and it has approached the necessity for producing a very large supply of technical experts in a straightforward way.

The general educational climate in Soviet Russia today is as scientific as the English educational climate was classical in the past. From fourteen to seventeen, everyone in the secondary schools studies physics, chemistry and mathematics, spending forty per cent of his time on these subjects. After the examination at seventeen, most of the bright young people appear to go almost automatically into the scientific institutes and divisions of the universities. The scientific courses last five years in the universities and almost throughout contain a literary element. Generally this is a foreign language, with history or literature sometimes in addition. This is also true of the four-year *technicum* course. We believe that one cannot go any distance educationally in the U.S.S.R. without some familiarity with a foreign language. This may be partly due to the fact that many of the textbooks and reference sources are in other languages. This means that the Soviet scientist is already prepared to take advantage of scientific developments reported in other languages.

The number of qualified science teachers in Russia is now estimated at something over a quarter of a million persons. That figure should be compared with less than 20,000 in Great Britain and less than 50,000 in the United States. This is all the more significant since this particular group of teachers appears to be very enthusiastic about its work and enjoys high status, considerably higher, for example, than that of the medical profession.

The channeling of so large a ratio of the educated into the scientific and technical professions takes on, we think, something of the character of a "crash" operation. This results in an overconcentration in the higher echelons in the scientific group, with the result that there are not enough competent people left to do the medium level jobs and the more ordinary technical tasks.

Persons who have completed higher education and who enter teaching, academic or scientific research careers are permitted to enter advanced training-research, which leads to two types of advanced degrees: a lower degree called "Candidate" and a higher degree called "Doctor." Three years are required to achieve the lower degree and four years are required to qualify for the higher degree.

Advanced degrees may also be awarded, like honorary degrees in this country, for certain achievements such as published works, scientific performance, and so on.

There are two levels of teacher training: the normal school and the university. The normal school level approximates the general pattern of secondary professional education such as is given nurses and semi-professional technical workers. We were told standards have consistently risen for semi-professional education, and our impression is that the present normal school-trained teacher would have the equivalent of at least two years of college in the U. S. The university level of training involves attendance at a pedagogical faculty of a university or at a pedagogical institute.

Continuous education of the teachers is emphasized. They are required to attend seminars during the summer vacation. At the present there is considerable discussion on retraining teachers for the newer emphases in the new ten-year curriculum to be discussed in the next chapter.

Teachers are expected to do considerable work after class hours, visiting the homes of the pupils, conducting parents' meetings, and working to bring the family and the school closer together.

The beginning salaries of teachers in the elementary schools are quite low. A figure of only 650 rubles per month was reported. They do gradually rise, however, to as much as 1,500 rubles and the median is between 1,100 and 1,300. Well-placed university professors may get as much as 3,000 to 5,000 rubles per month. The Soviet press contains many references to teaching as an honored profession and a teacher may be awarded a series of titles such as "Honored Master of Vocational Education."

Responsibility for research in the theory and practice of education is in the hands of the Academy of Pedagogical Sciences of the Russian Republic, the National Pedagogical Research Institute, and the higher pedagogical schools. We visited the Academy of Pedagogical Sciences and talked with the director; we also spent some time at the Pedagogical Research Institute. Both of these institutions are in Moscow.

While organized as an institute of the Russian Republic, the Academy by agreement serves all other republics which do not have comparable institutes. It is responsible for the development of manuals for teachers in all fields of education. These cover the teaching of individual subjects like reading, writing, arithmetic and natural sciences. It is the Academy that developed the new ten-year curriculum that went into effect in 1955. As another example of the scope of its responsibility, it is the Academy that was expected to develop in detail the regimen and specific educational curriculum for the new boarding school which will be discussed in the next chapter.

The Research Institute, which is associated with the Academy, maintains a variety of laboratories covering the psychological, acoustical, phonetic and visual aspects of education as well as laboratories for the design of mechanical instruments for the education of the handicapped child.

The Academy recently has been criticized both at the Twentieth Congress of the Communist party and in the public press. *Pravda* published an article in which the president of the Academy admitted to many failures and shortcomings of the institute. The general charge he conceded is that pedagogical science is still lagging behind life and the growing requirements of the schools and the teachers; the most important problems are being solved very slowly. Insufficient study is made of pedagogical experience, and the scientific generalization of such experience is not yet sufficiently clarified to be useful in pedagogical research. What emerges is that the broader responsibility of the pedagogical field for psychological knowledge and methods of conditioning the child's learning and growing up is not fully being met.

One of the more stimulating and inspiring incidents in our visit to Soviet Russia was the observation of some of the basic experimental work being done at the Pedagogical Research Institute on the re-education of the blind and the deaf. We were very much impressed with the caliber of the professional personnel engaged in this activity, their knowledge of methods in other parts of the world, and the relative freedom for experimentation which they are enjoying in their pioneer work.

A great deal of special research has been done here on the acoustical aspect of speech. This is consistent with the great emphasis we encountered in the psychiatric clinics on speech disturbances and speech problems (*locopedia*).

Most dramatic was the work reported to us by one of the research specialists at the Research Institute who has devoted a lifetime to the development of methods for educating the Helen Kellers of this world. It is our impression, which we have verified since our return to this country, that this scientist has gone very far in developing specific mechanical devices for teaching deaf and blind children. He told us he is able to teach such children how to speak in a manner which can be understood by others. This is an extraordinary achievement. He has also developed a number of mechanical devices which enable the deaf and blind to communicate more directly with speaking persons. One of his less complicated machines enables the blind to read the printed page without translation into Braille. A combination of photo-electric cells *scans* the page and communicates a pin-prick sensation to the fingertip such as is felt in reading Braille.

This experimental work seemed to us far beyond what we are doing in the same field at this time in the United States.

The major portion of Soviet education of blind children and adults is conducted in residential schools as it is done in England. Soviet adult blind are employed in special shops, largely maintained by associations of blind people. The blind are able to work at machines and do other productive work, but their employment is almost entirely limited to enterprises exclusively for the blind. As far as we could learn, they are not included to any extent in regular workshops and factories.

Mentally defective children are classified into three groups: the debiles, or mentally retarded children who can finish elementary school; the imbeciles, who can go as far as the fourth class, roughly the fifth grade in the United States; and the idiots, who are the non-educable mentally defective children.

The Russians, as we have indicated earlier, do not rely on the usual intelligence tests, such as the Binet-Simon or the various modifications and elaborations of the principles incorporated in that test. Instead, they rely on more comprehensive and less formal methods of observation by physicians, psychologists and teachers. Therefore, as far as possible, all children are sent to the regular public school for at least one year. If the child appears unable to meet the requirements of this school, he is studied for the causes of his failure, and in this study skills of teacher, psychologist and doctor are called upon.

These diagnostic procedures would seem to fully insure, more than is often true in sections of our own country, the adequate study of the children. The Russians are careful to distinguish the children who may fail in school but who are not intellectually limited from those who present problems of retardation. The latter may continue in the regular classes, being assigned less complicated work tasks than the usual pupils. Some are sent to agricultural schools or special schools located on the outskirts of the city where simple mechanical work is emphasized.

The imbecile child, after medical diagnosis, may require a special boarding school, under guardianship of the state, or he may be allowed to continue with his parents and attend a special day school. We were told by various authorities in the education and health fields that it is the general policy of the education authorities to leave children in their own homes as far as possible and to help the parents in the care and rearing of these children by special consultation and guidance.

Children classified as idiots become the responsibility of the Ministry of Social Security which conducts a number of colonies for mentally defective children. These are rural institutions. We did not visit any of them and have no additional information about them.

The basic policy for all educational activities—those of elementary and secondary schools as well as of all other forms and levels of education—is decided upon jointly by the Central Committee of the Communist party and the Council of Ministers of the U.S.S.R.*

Administration of the school system takes place both on the republic and on the over-all Soviet Union level.

The regular elementary and secondary schools are administered by the republic ministries of education, with local and regional branches exercising day-to-day operational controls over the schools. Curricula and methods of instruction are uniform for any given republic, and indeed for the entire

---

* *Soviet Professional Manpower*, p. 23.

U.S.S.R. Supervision of methods, programs of instruction and the activities of each of the fifteen ministries of education are co-ordinated by the Ministry of Education of the largest, the Russian, republic.*

Elementary and secondary school teachers usually receive their training in pedagogical institutes and teachers' institutes administered by the fifteen republic ministries of education, but supervised and co-ordinated by the Ministry of Higher Education of the U.S.S.R.

As distinct from elementary schools, the kindergartens may be operated by local economic enterprises, trade unions, collective farms and settlements. The ministries of education of all fifteen republics are responsible for standards and curricula, as well as supervision of the kindergartens, while the All-Union Ministry of Public Health supervises the physical education and medical care in the kindergartens as well as all activities in the nursery schools.

Job assignment takes place within five days after the issuance of the graduation certificate and the minimum term of assignment is three years. The opportunity for professional people to change jobs is limited. This restriction of job mobility, as well as differences in value placed on certain kinds of professions and occupations, weighs heavily with students in their choice of a field of training.

Although professionals of all types fare much better than any group of wage earners, there are still differential rewards for various occupations within the professional group. The favored professions and trades are within administrative managerial categories, scientific research, engineering and, in a declining scale, university teaching, medicine, and secondary school teaching.

A less obvious factor is the political hazard some professional and occupational fields, like biology, social sciences, and agri-

---

* Ibid., p. 10.

culture, carry with them. A change in public policy or party line may not only handicap a person in his career but may threaten him in more serious fashion.

As may be expected, there is great pressure toward the favored occupations with the result that establishments offering training for these have the greatest number of applicants.

In a previous chapter we have already referred to the general pattern of organization of the student body, as well as some of the functions the student council carries from kindergarten all through elementary school, secondary school and university. We have also referred to the parallel and somewhat different activities in focus and quality of the Young Communist League (Komsomol) and the Pioneers.

The Pioneers enroll children from the ages of nine to fourteen, and the Young Communist League between fourteen and eighteen. While enrollment is voluntary, the majority of pupils do belong to one or the other of these organizations. Both children and parents realize that such membership has advantages from the standpoint both of immediate reward and of future career.* Rewards include such things as two weeks of summer camp free, admission to special clubs and admission to puppet shows and movies at half price. Even more important, membership, according to general acknowledgment, heightens a student's chances of being admitted to a higher educational establishment or securing preferment in job assignment.

Some shift in the role these organizations play in the day-to-day operations of the school has taken place. Prior to the early 'thirties they interfered to a considerable degree in the work of the teacher and in school affairs. In recent decades their functions have been recast so as to aid, but not interfere with the teacher in maintaining discipline, in promoting learning and in co-ordinating extracurricular activities.

---

* Ibid., p. 42.

Because formal education through the school system carries far different implications in the Soviet Union than in the United States or Western Europe, we do not believe it is possible to make any comparison of the extent and character of extracurricular activities between these countries.

The Soviet regime places great emphasis on the importance of out-of-school activities as part of the educational, socializing and health building programs. The Official Report for 1955-56 reports the decision of the Twentieth Congress of the Communist party to expand the next Five-Year Plan facilities for children's out-of-school activities in towns and villages and "to secure a broader participation of clubs, palaces and houses of culture, engineering centers and other cultural and enlightenment institutions in educational work among school children."*

Sports occupy a leading place in the extracurricular activities. During the year 1955 a total of 1,000,000 pupils was said to have participated in various kinds of athletic competitions, the finals of which took place at an All-Union tournament for children held in Kiev during the summer of 1955. In addition to the summer tournament, winter skiing and skating competitions were held also.

Another phase of the extracurricular activities of children is education in aesthetics. Five thousand exhibits of the work of children were on display at the All-Union Children's Art Exhibitions held in the summer of 1956. A unique expression of extracurricular interests of children is exemplified in exhibition of children's technical inventiveness; these, too, are held on an All-Union basis. Skill in agricultural achievement is another art encouraged. Millions of children participate yearly in improvement programs in towns and villages and in the harvesting of crops. Prizes are awarded for outstanding results in plant culture and in animal husbandry. We have mentioned visiting a Pioneer camp for student agriculturists where a stay

* *Public Education in the Soviet Union,* p. 34.

of three weeks had been offered as an incentive in this field of extracurricular endeavor.

The relatively few children seen in the large cities during the summer is evidence of the government's program to send as many children and young people as possible to spend their holidays in the country. This program includes attendance at Pioneer and other excursion camps, children's sanatoria, walking tours, and visits to collective farms.

Keeping in mind Makarenko's emphasis on the part the family plays in the education of the child, it is to be expected that channels of communication would be set up by the schools to assure close relationships between the school and the family. Teachers have the responsibility of keeping in touch with families of pupils.

Another concrete medium of close relationship is the parents' association. While we understand there is considerable variation in the extent to which parents' participation is mobilized, the general pattern for such activities is through a parents' association and parent-patrons of the school.

The function of the parents' association suggests a superficial likeness to the parent-teacher association in our American school system. Parents meet with teachers regularly and these meetings serve to keep the parents informed of the general program of the class. They have a chance, also, to discuss their own child's progress with the teacher at this time. Certain members of the association assist the school as volunteers in helping parents whose children exhibit behavior problems in the school setting. Parents selected for this task are those whose own children are examples of model behavior. Children evidencing trouble in school may be considered victims of parental neglect; in such cases, the parents selected for this responsibility visit the home, try to counsel the parents of the problem child, and report back to the school. Parent-patrons are concerned with the provision of hot lunches for the children, with clothing, and so on.

In summing up, it can be said this comprehensive educational program, covering both children and adults and including both formal education and use of leisure time, is a remarkable example of planning in the field of human relations. Moreover, viewed quantitatively, the Soviet educational program has developed rapidly, incorporating extensive change in both scope and coverage. At the same time, the basic psychological assumptions and ideological objectives remain the same. Some of the developments which highlight this will be discussed in the next chapter.

XIV

Significant New Departures in Education

TWO IMPORTANT DEVELOPMENTS in Soviet educational affairs now under way bring into bold relief public policy with respect to the child. They are a product of the concern of the regime over the failure of the educational system to realize the goals set for it. This failure involves the kind of person which the educational system is producing, as well as his equipment for participating productively in accord with the changing demands of the social order.

These two developments—the introduction of the new ten-year curriculum and the establishment of the new boarding school—also bring home to us the inclusiveness of the concept of child rearing and education which is characteristic of Soviet ideology. The first, as we shall see, primarily emphasizes greater competence and mastery of skills; the second, the control of all aspects of the child's life as a requisite for the molding of his personality into the image which the state has projected.

The new curriculum is closely connected to the switch-over to universal ten-year schooling initiated in 1950. Achievement was to be gradual over the span of the fifth and sixth Five-Year Plans and to be completed in 1960. This means that in 1956 the country was in the sixth year of this transition.

Universal secondary education has already been introduced

in all the larger cities and considerable progress toward this goal is reported in the rural areas. That is to say, education is compulsory up to and including the seventh year for all children throughout the country. But in the larger communities, as necessary facilities are established, it is being made compulsory through the tenth year. Since 1950, when the new policy was introduced, the number of pupils in the eighth, ninth and tenth grades has increased by 4,300,000, or 3.45 the number at the beginning of the period. When the switch-over is completed it is estimated that the number of pupils completing the tenth grade will reach a high of 6,000,000, or double the number at the end of 1955.*

The effect of this new program, we were told by educators, will be to raise the admission level to the secondary semi-professional schools, as well as to materially modify the uniform curriculum for the ten-year school period.

In stressing the importance of the plan for universal ten-year schooling, the director of the Academy of Pedagogical Sciences brought out the following:

1. The universal requirements apply to all children, with the objective of having all children receive "a general and similar education" through the elementary and secondary school—in other words, in the years from seven to seventeen.

2. When the present program is fully implemented, admission to specialized technical and professional higher educational institutions will follow the completion of the ten-year program and not the seven years, as has been true heretofore for some of these specialized technical institutions.

The change-over to the ten-year program takes on much greater significance in the light of the new curriculum introduced in 1956.

"The greatest shortcoming" that existed heretofore "in the work of the school," according to the report of the Twentieth Congress, was "the partial breach between instruction and life, the inadequate training of school graduates for practical work."

---

* Official Report, 1955-56.

The new ten-year curriculum is designed to achieve the blending of the practical and the academic. The unusual emphasis on this is an admission that education at the elementary and secondary school levels heretofore has been traditional and primarily academic and sharply different from the technical or professional. "We are now striving to establish a polyvalent school, to incorporate within our program a polytechnical emphasis, but not technical as such: in other words, a training in basic vocational skills which will give children a basic preparation for technical education. We are eager to have the school prepare well-developed persons in all respects, to overcome the problem which lies in the difference between academic and technical and professional education. It is visualized that the 'technical' training may be given in some factory or other technical school. At the secondary school level we are introducing '*physical labor*' as such but not to the extent of interfering with academic education."

The important change that has been brought about is that previously the upper grades of the secondary schools prepared candidates primarily for the higher educational establishments. At the present time, the secondary school is supposed to prepare for "practical activities and freedom in the selection of occupation."

Before the switch-over to the ten-year program was introduced, most of the students entered the *technicums*, or semiprofessional training institutions, after seven years of education. They will now enter such institutions only after the completion of the ten years. The plan also is intended to prepare well-developed persons in all respects and to overcome the problem which stems from marked differences between academic and professional education.

The time allowed for vocational education in the new curriculum is approximately four hours per week out of a total of thirty-six. This is in addition to the sciences and mathematical subjects which have always bulked large, constituting almost forty per cent of the former total curriculum in the intermediate and secondary grades.

Geography and foreign languages are also emphasized much more than is usual in our own curricula. The study of geography is begun in the fourth grade and goes through the ninth. The emphasis on learning foreign languages is tremendous, including not only English, German and French, but also Chinese. Foreign languages are taught to all children beginning with the fifth year, or when the child is approximately eleven or twelve years old. In one military academy the teaching of foreign languages begins even earlier and there is a special elementary school in Moscow where all instruction for children eight years old and up is carried on in English.

The new emphasis on "polytechnization" is revealed in arts and crafts activities in the first four grades, in workshops where industrial plants provide the necessary equipment, in visits to neighboring plants, work on collective farms, and school experimental gardens.

Teachers are being re-educated to bring them into closer contact with practical work, with production methods and "closer to the present-day level of technology."

The introduction of the new curriculum with its new emphasis and the lifting of the general level of education opens many possibilities for the further expansion of specialized semiprofessional and professional education.

After the director had given me a detailed description of the new program, I asked: "Don't you think it may be difficult for some children to go through with the ten years of compulsory education? It may be too stiff for some."

His response, accompanied by a vigorous gesture, was: "We do not concede unequal abilities. In this we differ from the rest of the world. We hold that any normal child can take a ten-year education if all conditions are adequate." He added, with firm finality: "There will be a single uniform curriculum."

I realized, of course, that the leaders in Soviet education could not logically subscribe to any other theory. If they were once to accept individual limits, then they would face a major obstacle in building the ideal society because the contribution of some of the population would necessarily be limited or their ability might even be less than that necessary to function in a new society.

The Soviet thesis is that there are no limits to the educability of the normal individual. This is the premise which has led to a rejection of intelligence tests because such tests established the limitations of human capacity.

Another significant change in the present moves to extend education is the abolition in September 1956 of the fees of 150 to 200 rubles previously paid by the parents for their children's education in grades eight to ten. Imposed in 1940 and a part of the then emerging pattern of economic inequality, the fees were often provided in hardship cases by the local soviets or trade unions. However, their existence probably had some influence on attendance and their abolition represents part of the present program to increase enrollment in the upper grades.

By far the most significant step taken by the Soviet Union in the past decade, from the standpoint of basic philosophy of child rearing and education, is the establishment of the new boarding schools in the autumn of 1956. Our visit took place during the month before the schools opened and we felt some of the excitement of the new move in our talks with educators, newspaper people and others who understood the potentials of this step.

The decision to establish the boarding school had been made at the Twentieth Congress of the Communist party held during the spring of 1956. In September of that year, 170 such schools were ready to open in the Russian Republic. The plan had the blessing, we were told, of the highest leadership in the Soviet Union, especially, it is reported, of Khrushchev. Certainly it has far-reaching implications.

The *Report on Public Education in the Soviet Union,* which has been previously referred to, furnishes us with the reasons behind the establishment of the boarding school. "The family and the school remain, no doubt," says this report, "the most important nuclei of socialist education of children. But this can no longer be considered sufficient.

"In the past, in addition to the general schools, the ruling class had their own privileged system of educating the young generation, a system which corresponded to the existing regime and to the spirit of the time.

"Our socialist land is faced with the task of creating not an aristocratic caste, deeply inimical to the people, but builders of a new society, men and women of noble spirit and lofty ideals who will serve their people selflessly.

"These tasks of making child education incomparably better and more perfect are to be solved by the boarding schools.

"Children are to be enrolled in the boarding schools only at the request of their parents. They will live at the schools and their parents will visit them on holidays, during vacations or after school hours.

"Fine teachers equal to the lofty calling of engineers of the souls of the growing generation will be selected for the schools." (Italics ours.)

The report stresses the fact that the war left the country with a number of widows on whose shoulders has fallen the difficult task of bringing up fatherless children. There are also many families in which both parents work in a factory or office and are able to give only haphazard attention to bringing up their children. A considerable number of children are thus left to themselves and this not infrequently has serious consequences.

To begin with, each school will have ten classes, one for each grade, with thirty pupils in each. Later they may be enlarged to include twenty classes, or approximately 600 children. The educational curriculum will stress both general and polytechnical foundations for professional education. Adequate attention will also be paid to the aesthetic and physical aspects of the child's development and education.

Staffs will consist of both teachers and upbringers. For the first four grades, we were told, there will be one teacher and two upbringers for each group of thirty children. Grades four to seven will have one teacher and the equivalent of one and a half upbringers, with one teacher and only one upbringer for the remaining three grades.

The student organizations are expected to carry a higher degree of influence than ever in the new system. They are to help their fellow students in their studies, organize excursions and related activities, and give the pupils a sense of participation in the total life around them. They are expected to create a good group climate and good public opinion, but not to become the disciplinary arm of the school. The authority of the director is not to be supplanted.

This is a vastly more complicated administrative structure than any to which we are accustomed. It may prove difficult to achieve the necessary balance between the authority of the director of the school, the student council, the Communist party unit of teachers within the school, the parent organizations, the local Communist party units.

The new boarding school is visualized as serving two basic purposes—an ideal educational facility and an instrument for child protection. The boarding school is seen as a laboratory for the education of the ideal Soviet citizen of the future, and the source as well of answers to many of the educational problems which the ordinary elementary and secondary schools have been unable to solve to the satisfaction of the regime. Development of strength of character, initiative and creativity, motivation and dedication to Soviet ideals—these are but a few of the goals the new boarding school is expected to realize.

In addition to its function as an educational laboratory and demonstration project, the new boarding school is visualized as an important instrumentality for child protection and the rearing of children. It is interesting that in our interviews with leading educators, including the one primarily responsible for establishing these schools in the Russian Republic, there appeared to be some conflict between the purpose of education and the purpose of child care. So far, no balance seems to have been achieved between the emphasis on protection and the emphasis on the education of the ideal citizen.

Significantly enough, in describing the program of these schools, emphasis was laid on the fact the educational authority would be able to plan and control more completely the child's total experience during the whole of the twenty-four hours of the day. This is in contrast to the old boarding schools in the Soviet which simply provided care for the child and counted on the elementary school to provide the education.

In the light of this desire to control more completely the child's total experience and learning, the boarding school may be seen not merely as a new school, but as the beginning of a new system of child rearing. The question is whether or not the new schools are ultimately to supplant the child's own home and the ordinary public school. Despite affirmation of the importance of the family and the regular school as the nuclei of child education, articles in the press and the conversations we had with school authorities both indicate that if these schools prove successful they can be expected to supplant the ordinary elementary school. This would mean that children between the ages of seven and seventeen would be with their own parents only during vacation.

One cannot forecast how this issue will be resolved. The success of the schools will be one determining factor. The attitude of parents and their readiness to place children for as long a period as ten years will be another factor. The chances are that for a number of years the boarding schools will increase in number but are not likely to supplant the home and the ordinary public schools to any great degree.*

* The meeting of the Twenty-first Congress of the Communist party early in 1959 reaffirmed as a major objective the ten-year curriculum and the boarding school program.

XV

Does the System Work?

AS ONE STUDIES the comprehensive and complex apparatus the Soviet Union relies upon for rearing children and conditioning social behavior, the crucial question persists: does it work?

How far has external pressure to conform and behave in goal-directed fashion been successful? Has the system succeeded in mobilizing human energy for the common purpose? Has the sought-for harmony between individual impulse and social control been established?

In other words, is the U.S.S.R. producing the ideal citizen which the formulae are intended to achieve? Or is there evidence of nonconformity, of protest or rebellion against social demands? The answer, without doubt, is that there is. Even Soviet leaders admit that they have failed to achieve the full degree of participation and conformity by its citizens, and their deep concern is reflected in official reports and countless articles in the Soviet press. No society has been wholly successful in making human beings what they could be. But because of sweeping Soviet claims, "hooliganism," alcoholism, crime, juvenile delinquency, as well as mental illness (to the extent that it is reactive to environmental pressures), must all be regarded as symptoms of failure in the Soviet system of social control. Moreover, these problems occur in sufficient gravity to spur the regime to intensify its search for more effective methods.

While we ourselves had almost no experience with the phenomenon, probably because we traversed only the better sections of the cities, the Russian newspapers constantly deplore what they call "hooliganism." This diffuse term for aggression and social disrespect—rowdiness, insulting people on the street, pushing and jostling passers-by—seems especially anachronistic in the context of the Soviet social scene. It may, therefore, have some unique significance.

With statistics unavailable it is difficult to say whether alcoholism is greater in the Soviet Union than in other countries. But if, according to Russian theory, alcoholism is the result of tensions of living, there should be none in the newer generations of a socialist state. Yet we encountered a good many drunken men, usually arm in arm, and a lesser number of women. A striking phenomenon we frequently saw was drunken boys of fourteen and fifteen. We saw policemen speak to some of these boys, but none were arrested.

Drunkenness is not a crime in the U.S.S.R. and no one is arrested for it, but the government has done various things to discourage alcoholism. Wine, beer and liquors can be purchased only in package stores or in eating places where food is consumed with the beverage. The price of eighty-proof vodka—25 rubles for half a liter, two days' pay of the average worker—is in itself prohibitive. *Pravda* and other newspapers frequently carry articles deploring the spread of drunkenness and reporting therapeutic and rehabilitative measures that are being adopted to deal with the problem.

The Russian newspapers have made much of the "gilded youth of Moscow" and their indulgent and pampering parents. These young people are described as irresponsible, self-indulgent, pleasure-seeking, occasionally vicious and parasitical in that they live off their families and are unwilling to work. Apparently a large enough number exists to justify attacks in nation-wide publications.

Leaving aside for a moment the deeply troubling problem of delinquency which we shall discuss in the next chapter, another manifestation of nonconformity seemed to us to have greater significance than these gross manifestations. We refer to the attitudes of many young Russians brought up in the new society, who yet are in conflict with it. At least a half-dozen young men, hearing us speak English on the streets, in parks or subways, picked up conversations with us. They were students of English or young professional men who spoke English. Our conversations with these young persons were direct and informal, without intervention of an Intourist interpreter. They provided the freest exchange we had during our visit.

It goes without saying that we do not know how far the attitudes of the small number with whom we conversed were representative of the attitudes of others. Nor could we tell how far their protest was a product of their own personal experience. They established for us the fact that dissent does exist and that some young people felt strongly enough to take the personal risk involved in unsanctioned association and conversation with foreigners from the United States.

The protest of these young people covered a wide range of aspects of life in the Soviet Union today. A few targets of their scorn were the rigidity of the bureaucracy as seen in hospital visiting rules, assignment of living quarters, continued difficulty in getting food supplies, a series of discomforts in living including job assignments and inflexible conditions of work, lack of joy in life, overemphasis on stern ideals, absence of fun. They had a craving to talk about clothes, books, art, American jazz and current musical shows like *My Fair Lady*. They even expressed strong disagreement with the immutability of communist ideology and they scorned party membership.

In contrast to the protest of these young people, which is coupled with dissatisfaction with Communist parents, is the conflict which reflects some residue of the parents' own resistance to the present ideology. There are still educated families, "carry-overs" from the past, who continue to make an unfavorable comparison of their present life with the freer intellectual life in the past. Their views are transmitted, consciously or unconsciously, to the young.

At dusk one evening we were standing looking in the window of one of the better shops on the wide Nevskiprospekt in Leningrad when a voice said: "You are Americans?"

We turned and saw a tall, thin, almost skinny fellow of about twenty-five, with a homely, engaging, friendly face. It developed that he just wanted to practice the English he had learned in school. We talked a long time.

His name was Peter. Both parents were professional people and he himself was a chemical engineer. He lived at home with his parents and young brother who, Peter said with pride, was attending the university. They were well off, each earning from 800 to 1,200 rubles a month. The family enjoyed the luxury of a two-room apartment for the four of them and owned a TV set, a washing machine and an electric refrigerator. They had purchased these labor-saving devices for the sake of the mother.

"I hate to see her go out to stand in those long marketing queues after working all day," said Peter.

We gathered his work might be with atomic energy in some form. When we said, "You have a wonderful country here," he countered quick as a flash with: "Am I supposed to be grateful just because they give me a liter of milk a day to keep me going because my work is hazardous and they need me?"

Finally we parted and Peter asked if we would meet him the next evening. He had a strong desire to practice English, and he wanted to bring his chum along who also liked to practice English.

During our second meeting Edith asked if he had told his parents he was meeting an American couple for the second time.

"Tell *them*?" asked Peter incredulously, "You don't seem to understand. They are old-line Communists. They are party members. I *couldn't* tell them, they wouldn't understand."

"Aren't you a party member?" I asked.

No, said Peter, he was not. When "Uncle Joe" was alive, working people were not encouraged to join; membership was largely restricted to the elite.

"Now they want working people, but I don't want to join," he said. Pressed for a reason he said: "Many reasons. You are under surveillance a whole year. You must not drink or have fun. After you are allowed to join the department branch, then you must wait another six months to join the section group, then additional delay before you are admitted to the district group, then delay again to join the regional group. It takes years before you are a full-fledged member and all the time you are under surveillance."

"How about the union?" I asked. "Do you belong to the union?"

"Oh yes," Peter said. "While membership is voluntary it is foolish not to join the union. You lose too much if you don't. Union members get more liberal sick leave, better rates to summer rest homes, longer vacations. So every one joins."

After a half-hour, Peter's chum, Nick, arrived. Nick was a jaunty, handsome, Liliom-like individual. He regarded the world as his oyster, even the Soviet world, and he threw his weight around accordingly. While he never criticized the regime in any specific way, the tenor of all his remarks indicated his lack of identification with the powers that be.

Nick lived with an aunt who had been hospitalized for a heart attack. On his day off he went to see her, only to be told this was not a visiting day. "I demanded to see the superintendent," said Nick, "and I said, 'Are you here to serve people or to impose restrictions on them?' I got in. And then I went to the housing bureau and told them my aunt could no longer climb four flights. They gave us rooms on the ground floor. They don't push me around, I tell you," said Nick with great relish.

These taunting, cynical, young men were clear evidence that a generation reared in the Communist period and even in a Communist home still were able to dodge their way between propaganda and reality. They came a third time to visit with us but we missed them, much to our regret. Because of their fears, messages and further communication were not possible.

Another evening we were walking in a park in Moscow. It was still daylight. A well-dressed and self-assured young man approached us and said in German:

"Are you from Israel?"

"No," we replied, "we are from America."

With him was a beautiful young woman, blonde, with an oval face and the most vivacious eyes we ever saw. She was dressed with unusual elegance and carried herself with a poise and charm that were understandable when we learned she was B———, a well-known dancer. We strolled and talked together in Yiddish and German.

Food was plentiful, the young man said, clothing in short supply and housing bad. He told us much about the plight of Jews: how many of them had been downgraded in their trades and professions; how they met discrimination in many of their personal relationships. He also told us how this has sustained the consciousness of a separate identity.

The man was an engineer, he told us. "The safest thing is technical work, no politics . . ."

They were on their way to a party and we walked with them for more than an hour. We told them how much we wanted to visit a Russian home and they at once invited us for the next night. Unfortunately, we were leaving the city the next day and so lost our one opportunity.

One may well ask how the expression of protest by these young people can be reconciled with the schooling in loyalty to country and regime so assiduously carried out in all social settings. We do not have the answer and we must remember that dissent, in the Soviet Union as in other countries, is part of the adolescent process. (It is during adolescence that the young person begins to see differences between the glamorized version of living that he has been taught and the realities around him.)

Because of the character of Russian child rearing, adolescence in the Soviet is reported to come later than in our country. It takes place at a time when young people have acquired at least a little information about other countries and want more.

Hunger for news which we encountered among many persons to whom we spoke may not be altogether an expression of dissent, but it certainly reflects dissatisfaction with the supply of information about the outside world. The Soviet newspapers carry very little news as such. News is dealt with only in the context of comment, so that the Russian population, including the intellectuals, is cut off from objective reports of what is happening in the rest of the world.

We found among those who could read and speak English a strong interest in current American periodicals. While it was true one young man was frightened when we offered him a copy of *Time* in the subway, another begged for a copy of the current *Time* which we had with us and for any American books we might have. Still a third said he read a news magazine in the library of his school.

We learned that the American literature made available to and urged upon young people included Jack London, Hemingway, Jerome K. Jerome, Mark Twain and Howard Fast. None, not even the most literary young people we met, had heard of Eugene O'Neill or William Faulkner. All of O'Neill's plays are listed in the Lenin Library in Moscow, however, and this leads to speculation whether obstacles may not be put in the way of access to certain English language books. Orwell's *1984,* for example, is not in the catalog of this library, though his *Homage to Catalonia* is. When we raised the question of accessibility with the librarian in charge, we were told that certain books are in a special scientific section and are available to students showing a passport as evidence of their right of access.

One young man we met had known English from childhood and very much wanted to own a copy of the abridged Oxford English Dictionary. The official price is 400 rubles ($100.00). After much search he obtained a secondhand copy for 100 rubles.

Manifestation of interest in foreign literature, art, science, education or systems of thought appears to be dangerous in spite of so-called de-Stalinization. The fear of being branded "cosmopolitan" was present in most of our Intourist guides. But in spite of the cordon of restriction and disapproval, the thirst for firsthand knowledge of the rest of the world is so strong that a young architect, who in all other ways appeared to conform to Soviet social standards, in speaking of his work said passionately: "But I *must* travel! I *must* see Rome, Paris. I *need* this to be a good architect!"

Since protest does exist, you may ask what channels there are for the expression of criticism. And how actively and constructively are they utilized?

At the moment, correspondence in the public press is a sanctioned medium for public criticism. Letters are published which not only scold those who fail to conform to public policy and expectations, but also criticize those whose sins of omission result in injury or suffering of others. Criticism may be aimed at the chairman of a collective farm who misuses his office, the manager of a plant who has instituted unfair working conditions, the head of an industrial trust in a distant community who has failed to complete construction of badly needed housing for his workers.

A father voices indignation at the way the faith of his eight-year-old daughter has been undermined in the school she attends. Some of her fellow pupils, candidates for office in the student council, were notorious for their dishonesty and unprincipled conduct. Nevertheless, their names were placed in nomination and speeches describing them as paragons of childish virtue and integrity were made.

"What kind of morality is this?" cries the father who is understandably outraged because the teachers not only aided and abetted proceedings but actually helped write the false speeches. "This kind of education," he concludes, "can only bring up young people to serve a dishonest bureaucracy."

Another letter, signed by a committee of employees of a plant behind the Urals in far-off Asia, reports a desperate situation. No heating system had been installed in the plant since it had been established three years earlier although the equipment was delivered soon after the plant was built. For two winters the workmen had suffered and production during the winter months had been seriously reduced. Worst of all, the failure to meet production quotas had meant resultant loss of wages and the men had had little to eat.

Thus, a variety of lesser officials may come in for attack, but the regime and its basic policies are never criticized.

The cartoons in *Krokodil,* characterized by withering and bitter satire, are perhaps the most tangible examples of release for the irritation and annoyance of the individual at the prevailing social scene.

Some machinery for expression of dissent is available, according to some of our official informants, in the many kinds of organizations in which individuals are urged to participate: the sports clubs, parent associations, volunteer committees of the labor unions, school patrons, tenant committees.

I asked Professor Tadevosien, leading authority in the field of civil law, how the amendment to the Juvenile Court Law, raising the age of "limited responsibility" from fourteen to sixten, was initiated and brought about. He replied that it was enacted, like all other laws, by the Supreme Soviet. When I pressed him on how the desirability of the change was first expressed, who was responsible for its advocacy, and how it finally got on the agenda of the Supreme Soviet, he was hard put to it to give me a specific answer. He said that a suggestion for a change in law might originate within any "organ"—within a labor union or a local soviet—and then might be passed on to the next higher "organ," and in this way ultimately reach the Supreme Soviet.

The process which we know in our country—the advocacy of proposed legislation by a great variety of voluntary special or general interest groups and associations, including government departments at all levels, and accompanied by a great deal of public discussion—did not seem part of the processes in the Soviet Union.

However, the original draft of the recently enacted pension law was published in Soviet newspapers two months before its enactment, and provision was made for local hearings. Old people were invited to present their views; newspapers invited letters suggesting improvements. When the law was enacted, the president of the U.S.S.R. drew attention to the extent of the public discussion which had preceded enactment.

We never did get a clear picture of the process by which change in goals and methods is clarified and implemented. We were told over and over again that the final decision is that of the Supreme Soviet.

There is sufficient evidence to justify the assumption that the leaders of the Soviet Union have found that basic human emotions cannot be entirely ignored. Concessions have had to be made to satisfy human needs and striving and there is evidence of a continuing trend in this direction. The vision of the perfect state, honors for those who conform, fear of punishment—apparently none of these have proven sufficiently strong incentives to achieve the complete contribution of the individual to the common good.

Makarenko waxed romantic about the ideal Soviet family, free from greed and selfish interests, completely at one with the purposes of the state. Apparently it has proven difficult to sustain this kind of ideal human institution and so we find new sanctions: unequal rates of pay, ownership of personal belongings, homes and automobiles, and even the right of inheritance.

The shift in the relative responsibility for child care from community to parent may have represented something more than a wish to improve the quality of the child-rearing function. It may well have been a concession to the positive feelings of parents for their children.

Many of the measures recently adopted or projected may be regarded as further concessions to human needs: the shorter work-week, a more generous social insurance scheme, steps toward greater differentiation in the social roles of men and women, removal of women from the hardest and most hazardous occupations, and encouragement of femininity through an increase in the availability of beauty aids and ornaments.

But despite these cracks in the monolith, the general pattern is one of resistance to any basic change in public policy. This is true even though serious difficulties have been encountered in achieving the original goals. There is continued insistence on a certain image of the ideal personality although efforts to achieve it have failed and have engendered anxiety on the part of parents and educators. Rather than re-examine the concept itself to see whether it should be modified, rather than reappraise the practical possibilities of achieving this goal, the reaction of the regime to this failure is to blame parents and teachers and various social organizations, including the Communist party itself. The decision of the regime in the spring of 1956 to establish the new boarding school, described in Chapter XIV, is a concrete example of rigidity in the social process.

XVI

The Child Who is Delinquent

CONTEMPORARY THEORIES of social behavior and control hold that crime and delinquency are evidence of maladaptation between the individual and the social demands of his environment. Misbehavior is the concrete expression of nonconformity and rebellion. Studies of causative factors of delinquency among children in our Western culture—and this would be equally true of the Soviet Union—reveal a constellation of etiological factors which cuts across many aspects of the social order: economic, political, ideological mores and value systems. The increase of delinquency during periods of rapid social change or social dislocation is one proof of this.

It is our impression that responsible professional workers in the Soviet Union accept this thesis and are deeply troubled about delinquency and crime in their country. The first reaction to foreign inquiry is to deny its existence. "We had a good deal of delinquency after the war, but it is fast disappearing," they say. Confronted with the concrete fact of present-day delinquency, they respond that it is the result of faulty methods used by parents in child rearing or of irresponsibility toward offspring. Sometimes they further observe that the Soviet Union is still in transition toward the ideal social order it is striving to establish.

"As we improve our standard of living," said Professor Tadevosien, "we will reduce delinquency."

While professional workers in both America and the Soviet Union might agree that delinquent behavior represents an equation of individual and social factors, the way in which this equation would be elaborated in the Soviet Union would differ substantially from that in our own country. We would give much more weight to primary emotional factors—for example, to the relationship during the early years of life between the child and his parents. We would assume that the quality of this relationship and the way in which the child took adult values and patterns of response would determine his emotional growth. If the child-and-parent relationship is balanced and permits the child to grow up with a sense of being loved and protected, the chances are he will take on his parents' patterns of behavior. As these become part of his personality they will become the foundation for self-control and will condition his reactions to his experience as he moves from family to school and from school into broader community living.

We in the West see all behavior as purposive, as meeting the needs of an individual at a certain moment in his life experience. Delinquent behavior, too, serves some rational or irrational purpose. To state our idea about causation of delinquency very simply, we might say causation lies in a defective individual control system within a precipitating social situation. Put in other words, the delinquent is a youngster with certain unusual psychological needs facing a certain kind of life experience in which the delinquent act satisfies both his psychological and his rational needs. A classical example would be the young adolescent who engages in violent behavior like theft as a reassurance to himself of his masculinity as well as a means of material gain.

In contrast to this point of view about the causation of delinquency, the Soviet approach puts greater emphasis on learned behavior and almost none on the feelings of the child. Nowhere did we find any recognition that stealing might be a symptom of a child's emotional conflict. To them stealing is a product of insufficient or bad education that can be corrected by better education. The constant clamor in the Soviet Union is that children are improperly brought up, that parents do not set a good example, that they are not strict enough. The Russians put much less emphasis than we do on the failure of society to meet the need of the growing child and the adolescent in a wholesome way.

Where we would be concerned that our social institutions—the family and the school—provide the youngster with opportunities for expression of impulse, for experimentation, for creative experience and choice, the Soviet emphasis is on restraint, on the harnessing of impulse and directing it.

When we turn to treatment, our emphasis would be first, on emotional or psychological restitution, and, second, on reeducation; the first is to compensate for emotional deprivation and the second is to help the youngster achieve a more satisfying experience through the use of his talents. Both serve to help him gain a greater sense of adequacy. The Soviet approach is different in its emphasis on punishment and reeducation only, without any apparent awareness of the deeper emotional needs.

Those concerned with the problem of delinquency in the Soviet Union recognize that neglect of children may be a contributing factor. They recognize that a mother living alone and employed is handicapped in discharging her responsibility to her child. They also recognize that when both parents are employed they may be unable to pay sufficient attention to the needs of their child. They emphasize the importance of stabilization of the family and the role which workers' organizations, as well as the party, should play in establishing and regulating right relations between men and women. As we have seen, divorces are being discouraged, not only because of more stringent legislation but also because of public disapproval. Youth organizations and recreational centers must play a more important role; comic books have been prohibited. These are but a few indications of the direction of thought about prevention. They are very hopeful that the new boarding schools will help reduce delinquency.

As far as we can discover, little official information has been made available to the world at large about delinquency and crime in the Soviet Union. Delinquency is the prohibited area for the professional observer in that country. We have recounted our difficulties in making firsthand observations in this field. In the end, by dint of persistent pressure we were successful in getting to see many of the people and establishments that were pertinent to the understanding of the problem. We actually did see two judges of People's Courts, a People's Advocate, a professor who was an authority on civil law, an Assistant Procurator-General on the All-Union level, a children's inspector in the school system, two juvenile police officers, several educators and psychiatrists. And, to top the list, in the secluded Ministry of Internal Affairs I saw the official responsible for administration of the juvenile colonies, the reformatory institutions for children and youth.

As is true for other manifestations of social disorder, statistics are unavailable on the extent of child delinquency in the Soviet Union. Although the newspapers carry many stories of delinquent behavior by young people, the official position remains that both delinquency and homelessness among children were postwar phenomena only and have now disappeared.

Our personal observation was that except for the few drunken boys we saw and an occasional group of girls, much like American bobby-soxers, loitering around street corners in the early evening, children and young people on the streets and in the parks and youth clubs were unusually well behaved.

We tried to get an estimate of the extent of delinquency in a city like Moscow or Leningrad. Two judges of the district courts of Moscow said they had very few cases of children during the year in their courts. They pointed out that only rarely did they send children to rehabilitation colonies. A juvenile policewoman in one Leningrad district with a population of 25,000 estimated that she dealt with about six cases a year where the disposition was commitment to the colonies. On the other hand, the professor of civil law said from twenty-five to thirty per cent of all crimes are committed by children. The city of Leningrad has two disciplinary schools, operated by the

Office of Education, which care for about 300 problem youngsters each.

The case stories of delinquents appearing in the newspapers and those recounted to us by officials with whom we talked seem much like our own. While their theory is that delinquency is a product of deprivation, their own stories do not bear out this narrow interpretation. Examples cited more often involved privileged youngsters than underprivileged ones and the cause more often seemed to be pampering than deprivation. We encountered an anxiety of some educators that children from families of officials who carry unusual public responsibilities—and therefore have little time for their children—get into difficulties more often than those from simple homes.

One case described to us by a judge involved an eleven-year-old child of a relatively well-to-do family who stole candies and cigarettes from store counters and fountain pens in school. The behavior had persisted for some time and the mother herself told the judge that the child was beyond her control. After consultation with the teacher and the mother, the judge committed this child to a youth colony. There was no social or psychiatric study of the case beyond the conference between teacher, parent and judge.

Two kinds of courts and a children's commission, as well as the children's inspector and the juvenile police, have legal jurisdiction in delinquency matters. There is no special children's court in the Soviet Union.

In general, children under twelve are not brought into court but are dealt with by the juvenile police and may be committed to institutions with the consent of their parents. If a child under twelve commits a theft, the parents may be fined by the juvenile police or the child may be committed to an institution by the borough or regional commission for child protection.*

In Moscow a special commission, known as "The Commis-

* John N. Hazard, *Law and Social Change in the U.S.S.R.*, pp. 257-259.

sion for Providing Unmanageable Children with Work," was established in each region of the city during the war. The chairman of this body is the vice-chairman of the local soviet and the members include representatives of the education department, the police, the parents' association and the trade union. This commission may take note of girls wandering around at night or of boys who are idle, and may arrange for work for them or placement in an institution. I was advised that during the period when persons charged with political offenses were committed to prison by administrative tribunals and without trial, these commissions took over the responsibility for the care of the children of such imprisoned parents.

I have not been able to determine whether this commission is different in its responsibilities from the child care and guardianship commission referred to earlier, or whether it is merely different in name, whether such commissions follow a single pattern or vary between different cities and republics. I do know that commissions with similar powers did exist in the other cities we visited.

During the spring months of 1956 legal provisions governing juvenile crime were liberalized. Up until that time children under fourteen were only charged with limited criminal responsibility; they were not held responsible for crimes except rape, assault with knives, and crimes connected with individual dignity. From fourteen on they were held fully responsible. Under the new law of 1956 full responsibility does not begin until age sixteen.

The People's Court has criminal jurisdiction over all crimes except murder, banditry and political offenses. These latter are dealt with by the Supreme Court.

The People's Court is presided over by a judge and two assistant judges or "assessors"; two out of the three may pass sentence. The judge may be considered professional although he need not be trained in the law. He gives full time to his position as judge and has no other duties. The two assistant judges serve without pay and are selected from a panel elected by the votes of the district. They serve for a relatively short period, approximately two weeks. Each offender, whether child or adult, is represented by an advocate; the procurator represents the interests of the state. The law provides that children may be examined only in the presence of their parents.

Each region has one or more courts. One of the courts I visited served a population of 50,000. The courts are open to visitors and proceedings are comparatively informal. There is no probation staff and the burden of investigation falls either on the police officer who filed the complaint or on the court staff itself.

In Moscow there is a provision for sending the child to the Serbsky Institute of Forensic Psychiatry for study. More recently, children have been sent to regular psychiatric hospitals. If the recommendation, after psychiatric examination, is that the child be dismissed, the judge will usually follow the recommendation, although he has the right of veto if he sees fit.

Under Article 51 of the Criminal Code, the judge has the right to lessen the sentence for any offender if he considers the circumstances unusual. In the case of children, he may dismiss the case, release the child to his parents "on their word"; there is no probation officer, no regular reporting.

Judge Shuttava Izhdanov, of the People's Court in the Fourth Sector, Zarsinski district, Moscow, told me of one of her cases:

A fifteen-year-old boy whose father was dead was influenced by an older man living in the house to attack a man and take his clothing. When the boy was brought to Judge Izhdanov, she sent for the employer in the shop where the boy worked. He was reported to be a boy of good habits; this was his first offense. So the judge suspended the boy's sentence and sent the older man who influenced him to a labor camp. In arriving at a decision she had no help from a professional staff worker grounded in either social or psychological science. She made her own investigation and made a common-sense decision.

In every district, the police have one or more children's

police officers. They maintain a children's room which is used for holding runaway or lost children or other children until such time as the parents can come for them or they are placed in the detention home.

The children's police officer does not always wear a uniform and the ones I interviewed emphasized a moderate, informal approach to their responsibilities, with a great deal of stress on advising parents.

The children's police officer has the right to fine parents up to 200 rubles. Fines on parents may be imposed for the rudeness of the child, for traffic violations, riding on the back of a bus, or walking on the grass. In the case of complaints of children's behavior by the police officer, the juvenile officer visits the home, usually involving the chairman of the tenants' committee in her investigation. She may also report the behavior of the child to the plant where the father is employed, so that the officials there may urge the parents to do a better job.

If the offense is serious enough or the home unsuitable, the child is placed in the detention home where he may remain as long as a month, during which time the police and the officials of the home recommend to the court the disposition of the child. Teacher and parents are usually present at the court hearing.

The child may be committed to any of a number of different institutions: a home for neglected children, the disciplinary school under the supervision of the board of education, or one of the two classes of colonies—the educational colony or the work colony.

As I stated above, the Director of Youth Colonies in the Ministry of Internal Affairs described to me the program of a colony for delinquents. The colonies accept children between the ages of twelve and sixteen. The educational colony serves the neglected child and the milder delinquent. The work colony takes the more serious delinquent. The children may remain in the educational colony until they are about seventeen and in the work colony until they are eighteen, and sometimes nineteen. While the upper age for admission is sixteen, sometimes youngsters of seventeen may also be committed to the work colony. In the main, the children are committed to the colonies by the People's Courts, although they may also be sent there by the Supreme Court.

The school itself in the colony is described as much like a city school, providing education through the tenth grade. It is equipped with shops, which provide trade training. The day is divided, four hours in school and four hours in shops. Youngsters may begin to work at the age of fourteen; the law is strict that no child under fourteen may work. Those under that age may become acquainted with a trade but may not work regularly at it. The children also participate in the care of the institution, helping in the kitchen and gardens and in taking care of their dormitories and residences.

The population of a colony is usually about 300. The staff numbers approximately one adult for every two youngsters and includes academic teachers, vocational teachers, medical personnel and upbringers.

According to my informant, the youngsters do not feel they are in prison. They are allowed to visit in the city from time to time and are also allowed to work on the neighborhood collective farms. Parents are permitted to visit every few months. Some of the colonies are surrounded by fences, some are not.

A colony is like a small village; it consists of many buildings, schools, dormitories. Dormitories are not locked. Runaways occur, presumably not many. A child often comes back from a runaway voluntarily, but there is provision for the staff to look for them.

Considerable recreation is provided. Dormitories often put out athletic teams. There is usually a colony orchestra. They have drama and movies.

The distinction between the educational and work colonies largely lies in the fact that there is more emphasis on work in the latter; another distinction is that neither Pioneer nor Komsomol organizations are permitted in the work colony.

As to individual attention, I was told that if the child is unhappy he is expected to turn to the upbringer, who is supposed to know the interests and desires of the child. He helps him write letters to his family; if he is homesick, he persuades him to stay or, in an educational colony, he may arrange a leave for the child to go and see his parents.

Discipline is dealt with in the first instance by the counselor talking to the child; in the second, through group handling; in the third, through a *prekas*, a notice on the wall, spelling out the offense which the youngster has committed; and in the fourth, confinement to the isolation room. I was told that under no circumstances was corporal punishment allowed and that anyone who engaged in it was discharged.

The upbringers, or counselors, are mostly trained as teachers but not always. They may live on grounds or in the near-by town. There is a problem in finding suitable personnel.

Children are usually committed for a period of three years, but if the child makes good progress, he may go home much earlier—at the end of one year or even six months. The usual stay is approximately two years. Discharge is arranged through the committing court; the director of the institution makes recommendations to the court on the basis of the child's progress. The relationship between the director and the child may continue after he leaves, but there is no compulsion on the child to report.

This account of a trial for murder of an eighteen-year-old, which appeared in *Izvestia* on January 27, 1956, is worth quoting in its entirety because it brings to light many of the social problems entering into the control of delinquency and crime in the Soviet Union.

This is how it happened. On the evening of September 9th five boys, of whom only Romanovsky had reached eighteen, were idly wandering the streets of Kiev when they noticed an apartment in which the lights were on but no one was home. Setting lookouts, Romanovsky put his hand through the ventilation pane, reached down to the window lock, opened it and entered. After robbing the apartment, the thieves set out for the home of Burkovskaya, a woman of no known occupation, to cache their loot. The next day they sold the loot at the Zhitni Bazaar. Here Romanovsky bought a razor, although he had never shaved and did not intend to use it for shaving, since he threw away the razor case and began to whittle a twig with the razor.

That evening the thieves became drunk in May First Park, together with Burkovskaya and her girl friend Skarda. Evidently the boys soon grew unbridled, for the girls decided to slip away from them under cover of the darkness. Skarda succeeded by hiding in the bushes, but the boys caught Burkovskaya, threw her down in a flower bed and began to beat her.

At that moment three young men, walking in the park, saw that a woman was being beaten and hastened to the spot. When they approached Romanovsky and asked what was the matter, Romanovsky drew the razor from his pocket and, instead of answering, slashed Lt. Shcheglov's throat. The victim died in a few minutes.

Those are the facts.

There is much that is frightening in this incident. It is frightening that a person can silently walk up to another and suddenly cut his throat. It is frightening that he bought the razor deliberately and carried it on the ready in his jacket pocket. It is frightening that he was 18, an age at which most young men are writing poetry, building airplane models and falling in love for the first time.

Did Romanovsky grow up in bad surroundings and see only bad examples during his brief life? No. His parents are quite respectable people. His father is chief of a shop of the Kiev Machine Building Plant. His mother? What mother teaches her son to kill?

But had everything been done by family, school and Young Communist League to prevent the tragic end? No. True, the public school officials had once tried to influence the ruffian and had written to the party committee of the [father's] plant, but the comrades of the party committee had not even considered it necessary to mention the letter to the father. After all, why bother a Communist and distract him from his work for such trifles!

The Young Communist League? When Romanovsky was expelled from school and his father set him up in a job at the machine plant, the Y.C.L. committee of the plant did not even interest itself in why the lad did not transfer to the plant's Y.C.L. organization.

The father? When he learned a year ago that his son, a minor, had joined four comrades in raping a woman, the father rushed to the victim and offered her a bribe to drop the case against his son. She accepted. The father saved the rapists. But now, doubtless, he realizes that if he had not done this his son would have paid the penalty for his first crime according to the full penalty of the law, but he would not have become a murderer.

The case was hushed up, the shop chief's prestige was saved, and the plant's Y.C.L. committee washed its hands of the Young Communist Romanovsky, for whose deed it would have had to blush or even bear responsibility.

I cannot delve into the questions of school and family, the questions of upbringing and the prevention of crime by minors. The case of Romanovsky, unfortunately, is not unique, and one had to think not so much about re-educating the ruffian as about protecting the innocent passerby from the ruffian's knife. Occasionally one hears of youngsters becoming drunk and running amuck. A young man in a moving picture theater struck a girl across the eyes. A group of pupils of Public Schools Nos. 19 and 20 regularly attacked passing women and robbed them of their watches. One cannot fail to regard such cases with wrath and indignation, particularly since the offenders are often pupils who are good at their studies and well regarded in their families but cease to resemble humans when they are out on the streets.

Not long ago I read a newspaper article about hooliganism among youngsters. As a preventive measure, the author proposes holding more lectures for young people and issuing colorful posters. He thinks that interesting Young Communist League evenings are needed to attract young people.

No doubt all this is correct when one is speaking of the upbringing of young men and women. Young people certainly need romanticism, entertainment and innocent pleasures. Unfortunately, both family and school upbringing among us suffer from great shortcomings. There is much that we fail to do to organize good, cultured, entertaining recreation for young people. I repeat: I want to discuss only how to combat hooliganism when we have not succeeded in preventing it.

A stirring poster will hardly cause the ruffian to repent. Would it not be better to think about establishing a social atmosphere in which the ruffian would find himself in an intolerable position? These hearties are bold because they are confident that they can get away with it. They know that when they attack someone, passersby will act as though they do not see and the militiaman [policeman] will go around the corner in order to avoid having to intervene. If the ruffian does meet resistance, it is only from individual hardy souls, with whom he finds it easy to cope, not from *all* passersby, *all* the passengers in the streetcar, *all* the spectators at the motion picture, against whose united resistance the ruffian would be impotent.

Have measures been taken to put the ruffian in his place? Yes—but rarely. Articles have been written, decrees adopted. But most often the articles have been toothless and the decrees have simply not been carried out. For example, there was the decision of the Kiev City Soviet, which laid down a whole series of measures, including a 10 o'clock curfew on children under sixteen.

But this decree hung on the walls of buildings for a time and gradually disappeared. It was forgotten not only by those for whom it was written, but by those who had drafted it. In disregard for one of its provisions, minors can easily buy cigarettes and vodka.

Once I asked a salesman: "Why do you sell vodka to a boy?" "I have a sales quota. It's my business to meet the plan," he replied.

The salesman has a plan, and he sells boys vodka by this logic. But it appears that the militia also has a "plan" that sometimes makes the militiaman turn his back on an incident in the street.

Once I turned in a statement to the city militia concerning a robbery in my apartment. Several months passed, but I received no reply. I made a second approach to the militia administration. Digging in his desk, the representative of the detective force told me no such statement had been received.

I walked out, indignant. On the street a gray-haired militia official came up to me and said:

"Evidently they didn't succeed in catching the thief, so they threw your statement in the wastebasket."

"What do you mean—threw it out?"

"Every failure to catch a thief shows up in the statistics. If the precinct has a lot of failures, it's in bad repute. They have to drop such statements as yours in the wastebasket so as not to spoil appearances!"

No comment necessary, as they say. This kind of "'effort to meet the plan" is undoubtedly peculiar. Certainly it places prestige and advantage above public order.

It is hardly surprising therefore that when a gang was caught which had held up more than twenty Kiev citizens on the streets and had taken their watches, it appeared that not one of the gang's victims had even troubled to report the thefts to the militia. Was it worth reporting? They wouldn't find the thieves anyway.

Recently a friend told me of a disgraceful incident he had witnessed on a streetcar. A tipsy young fellow entered the car. Pushing his way forward, he noticed an old lady at the window. He didn't like her profile for some reason and declared that he wouldn't ride in the same car with her. Whereupon he began to shove her out of the car.

There were many people in the car. Yet among them there was none brave enough to face up to the ruffian. True, the conductor tried to argue with him. But when he saw that the obstreperous passenger held something in his hand resembling a safety razor blade, he promptly fell silent.

Upon hearing this story, I telephoned the militia precinct. I asked how this barbaric incident had ended. The militiaman on duty answered: "I know nothing about it."

There had been no militiaman in the streetcar and none of the passengers had even reported the incident, let alone stopped the ruffian. The militiaman on duty at the precinct was sincerely indignant at the passengers' failure to report and he was right.

Indeed, can one blame the militia in this case?

One more fact. The group of schoolboys who had held up passersby and taken their wrist watches sold the watches, in all twenty-two instances, through Kiev secondhand shops. All the watches were women's watches, many of them expensive ones. They were brought to the secondhand shops by young boys. Surely the officials of a state institution like a secondhand shop should have paid more heed to this circumstance in at least one instance. Why did they not report it to the militia? Certainly they could not have failed to realize that for a schoolboy to be selling a woman's gold watch is a strange situation!

Perhaps the secondhand shops have their plan, too, and any means is considered good which meets it.

Yes, the militia sometimes functions badly, but without support from the public and from each individual citizen it is often helpless. The borough executive committee's Commission for Combating Neglect and Lack of Supervision of Children does nothing. The volunteer aides of the militia do little to help the militia. In a word, the public merely makes demands of the militia but gives the militia utterly insufficient help.

Some cities have instituted the following system recently: anyone who indulges in swearing on the street pays a five-ruble fine on the spot, anyone who insults a passerby pays twenty-five, anyone who causes an uproar pays one hundred. In Krivoi Rog, for example, where hooliganism on the streets used to be common until recently, this simple measure brought splendid results.

Until the war Kiev had a twenty-four-hour people's court before which a ruffian could be hauled at any hour of the day or night for immediate trial. For some reason there is no such court now. But it is essential. Cities must have a place to which a ruffian can be dragged through all the streets for immediate sentencing. Unquestionably such a measure would help to stop ruffians and would cool the ardor of the criminals.

It is bitter to speak of all this, but one cannot be silent. A barbaric and wild appearance is created among Soviet people by the tipsy ruffian wearing a tiny cap, carrying a cigar in his teeth and staggering along in the embrace of others like himself, forcing everybody to make way in fright and disgust. Such persons must be met by the wrath of the public and made to feel the full force and severity of Soviet laws.

XVII

The Mentally Ill Child

OUR OBSERVATIONS about Soviet basic social purpose and orientation, and about family life, child rearing and education, as well as the organization of medical services, all serve to provide background for a consideration of mental illness among children and the treatment of the mentally sick child.

Children are either well or ill, and no one speaks of the "emotionally disturbed" child in the Soviet Union. Behavior problems short of illness are the responsibility of the education authorities and are dealt with by educational methods. The psychologically sick child is the responsibility of the medical authorities and is treated through medical facilities: clinics, dispensaries and a variety of inpatient resources. However, the division of all deviation in child growth and behavior within these two broad categories does not mean that environmental influences upon the development of the personality and mental health of the child are not recognized.

One of the leading authorities on mental illness in Soviet Russia, in a paper given at an international mental health meeting in 1954, pointed to a decline in the number of mental cases in the years following the war as compared to the higher incidence during the war years. While they cited no figures, the professional workers to whom we talked claimed there has been a decline in the incidence of mental illness among children. They said this was true not only for neuroses, which they claim have almost entirely disappeared, but also for such illness as schizophrenia and other psychoses.

We were on the alert for the usual signs of emotional problems—thumb-sucking and fearfulness, but did not find such symptoms any more prevalent than in our own children. We were told, however, that enuresis is common and persists until the early school years.

Although we could not get figures on the extent of mental illness among children, there are ways, we believe, of arriving at rough estimates of the problem. The number of children's departments in regional psychiatric dispensaries, the number of professional personnel employed in these departments, taken together with the length of time a case is in treatment, provide some clue to the volume of the outpatient load. Similarly, the number of beds in the different classes of inpatient facilities, taken with the figures on average length of time, provides a basis for another estimate. For example, one mental hospital for children has 250 beds and the average stay is three months, so that one could assume the hospital receives, on an average, one thousand new patients a year. One tentative conclusion is that while no exact comparison can be made between Russia and the United States with respect to the incidence of mental illness in children, there is sufficient evidence to show that the problem within the Soviet is a substantial one.

The Russians sharply differentiate the causative factors in neuroses from those of the psychoses. While the existence of neuroses among children is sometimes denied and sometimes reported as an insignificant and fast-disappearing problem, there is nonetheless some recognition that neurosis may be a product of maladjustment between individual capacity and social demands. However, while recognizing reactive elements, the Russians see them as injuries of the organism.

Neuroses, like other psychological illness, therefore, are interpreted as a basic dysfunction of the cortical process of stimulation and inhibition. Psychogenetic or functional factors, in the light of Pavlov's teaching, must be seen as secondary and not primary causative factors.

In the paper referred to above, delivered by a leading Russian psychiatrist at a recent international congress on mental health, the connection between life experience and neurosis is explained as follows:

The work of Pavlov's laboratories, he said, brought out the fact that the development and strengthening of the so-called dynamic stereotype—a recurrent group of responses to a uniform system of external stimuli—enhances and normalizes higher nervous activity. Readjustment of the stereotype presents much difficulty and sometimes may lead to experimental neuroses. These experimental data are directly relevant to the problems of mental hygiene.

It is common knowledge that for many individuals a change of habitual mode of life and occupation means great difficulties and may give rise to a neurotic state. These discoveries of the Pavlov school are also of great importance to teachers who work with children just entering school with their own home-developed dynamic stereotypes. The teacher is required to work out their new stereotype—to make them sit still at lessons, not to address their fellow pupils, etc.

By getting acquainted with the elements of the teaching on higher nervous activity, the wide public comes to realize that neuroses are no fatal thing, arising from the mystic depths of the subconscious, but a materially grounded phenomenon developing under fixed laws and cognizable by science—a certainly revertible and curable disease.

I. P. Pavlov, in summing up the results of his investigations, attributed great importance to training and gradualness in increasing the efficiency of nerve-cells. In clinical and pedagogical practice, Pavlov said, they should be held as guiding physiological principles. (Pavlov's *Wednesday*, vol. 2, p. 439).

It is clear, of course, that the same principles must be applied to mental hygiene, in solving the problems of increasing assignments for work or study, in scheduling time for work and recreation, etc.

P. V. Gannushkin, a foremost representative of the Korsakov school in psychiatry and a great expert in the so-called minor (child) psychiatry, said as far back as in 1933 that rationally organized social environments and the socialist mode of life, with its new organization of labor and new life conditions, prevent the development of psychopathies and lay the basis for the formation of a new personality. Twenty years have passed since then. Life has wholly confirmed Gannushkin's prophecy. The practice of our hospitals and clinics reveals an unfailing decline in the number of psychopathies occurring in the Soviet Union.

The facts of reality give proof to the correctness of Pavlov's principle of the unity between the organism and its environment, of the decisive influence of social surroundings on the development of personality.*

Psychoses in children, we were told again and again by the Soviet psychiatrists, are the product of "residual meningeal diseases" and other post-infections—such as, meningitis, encephalitis, and poliomyelitis. They are also the result of brain damage and other forms of organicity. Upon some questioning by us, it was granted that some school phobias did exist. Also we learned that the school program may prove too burdensome for some children and adjustments have to be made; after the school year some children may be sent to a sanatorium for a special rest.

We made some attempt to learn about diagnostic methods and classifications. We concluded that no comparison between the methods employed in our own country and in the Soviet Union in the treatment of mental illness would have validity unless a clinical team were to make a full study of a number of individual cases.

Another observer whose notes were available to us secured a classification of types of disorder from two leading psychiatrists in Moscow for the year 1954. One was a table classifying patients in a local hospital, the other a similar table for all patients in the Soviet Union. The classifications did not correspond. One used categories such as hypertension, war trauma, war veterans, while the other used such categories as diseases of the central nervous system. Both used the five standard categories: schizophrenia, epilepsy, neurosis, manic-depressive and syphilitic psychosis, but these covered only about forty to fifty per cent of the total patients classified.

---

* Professor O. V. Kebrikov, *Principles of Mental Hygiene and Prophylaxis and the State of the Mental Health of the Population in the U.S.S.R.*

I myself read a few cases of the children. The social histories, while not as lengthy as in some of our own clinics, were substantial and provided considerable information about the parents and the general family situation. In the case of a nine-year-old child of retarded development and very fearful, the mother, a teacher, was said to be tense and impatient; there were differences about the handling of the child between the mother and the grandmother who lived in the home. But these social facts were not utilized in arriving at the diagnosis or in the plan of treatment. The child was diagnosed as schizophrenic.

Another case was that of an eight-year-old boy who suffered from disturbed sensory functioning; among other symptoms he had diplopia. He was diagnosed as a case of organicity. However, the treatment recommended did not seem to be specifically related to the diagnosis. It consisted of vitamins, sedatives, a general regimen within a residential setting, with emphasis on education.

Many of the children at the Central Psychiatric Dispensary in Moscow which we visited suffered from speech disorders. We were permitted to see one of the therapists, who was not a physician, treating one of the children. This child was described as originally fearful and oppositional. Treatment consisted of speech exercises in front of a mirror. The material used consisted of children's stories and the child was stimulated to speak by a series of little storytelling cards. The mother was present during the treatment session.

Psychiatric services are an integral part of the general medical facilities and include outpatient day treatment and a variety of inpatient arrangements. Psychiatric problems are discovered early through the polyclinic or general health clinic. As we have seen, a psychoneurologist is included among the specialists on the staff of the polyclinic.

Individuals or families who are troubled about child behavior or manifestations of mental illness may, in the first instance, go to the polyclinic or to the specialized regional psychiatric dispensary, which may be housed with the polyclinic. After the child is seen at the dispensary and a diagnosis has been made, he may continue to come to the dispensary for treatment on an outpatient basis.

In addition to the contacts with a psychiatrist, the family may be visited by the social or patronage nurse. She carries a wide range of responsibilities, concern with the environmental situation of the child, with his work at school and the way he is managed at home by his parents. She also deals with such matters as housing, special financial assistance in case of need, or guardianship problems. In other words, she may combine the duties of a caseworker in a family agency, a psychiatric caseworker, or a visiting nurse. She does not have any special training, however, except supervision which she receives from the psychiatrist in her work.

In addition to its direct treatment responsibility to those who apply or are referred to it, the special psychiatric dispensary also provides treatment and observation of patients discharged from mental hospitals. It recommends children for special disciplinary schools conducted by the educational authorities, selects children for admission to day sanatoria or day treatment centers, or commits patients to acute or long-term mental hospitals.

Inpatient facilities in the Soviet Union are differentiated according to the functional focus as well as between children and adults. The day sanatoria for children, similar in function to the Child Development Center in New York City, are intended for children of preschool and early school age who may find it difficult to attend a regular school. The plan provides for smaller groups and more individualized approach than is provided in the ordinary school. The children remain only for the school day and return home at night.

Then there are children's departments in mental hospitals for those children and adolescents whose illness is in the beginning stages and considered acute. When the illness passes into the protracted stage, the patients are transferred to mental hospitals for the chronically ill, which are usually located in the country and are referred to as "colonies." There are also institutions for the mentally defective under the Ministry of Social Security.

The disciplinary schools, operated under the Ministry of Education, represent another form of treatment situation. These are for children with learning problems or some milder forms of neuroses, and for those who have committed the less serious delinquent acts.

During our visit we had the opportunity of observing a day treatment center, and a residential unit for 50 younger disturbed children, connected with the Central Psychiatric Dispensary in Moscow, as well as the children's department of a mental hospital with 240 beds. The physical facilities were informal and the physical standards adequate. In the unit which was part of the Dispensary the dormitories were small, containing about six beds each. In the hospital unit the dormitories were much larger, accommodating approximately 12 children each.

In the larger unit, the children's department was located at some distance from the adult hospital and consisted of a number of separate buildings. It was divided into sections based on sex, behavior, and manageability: quiet, semi-restless, and restless. Each section had classrooms and play rooms in addition to dormitories.

What was impressive was the ratio of professional and nonprofessional personnel to the number of youngsters. This was high in both facilities, with at least one staff member per child. The ratio of psychiatrists to the rest of the staff was much greater than usually found in residential centers in our own country. We were told that one of the centers has one psychiatrist to every ten child patients. The quality of competence, adequacy and warmth displayed by the staff toward the children could not help but evoke our admiration and respect.

Treatment is carried out through a wide range of intervention and therapy at the social, educational, medical and psychological levels, from rest to gymnastics, from sleep to shock therapy.

As a means of achieving some rationale for the wide variety of therapeutic efforts, we have classified treatment methods in the Soviet Union under four different headings:

1. The raising of general health and body function to its highest level including such measures as vitamins, diet, rest and gymnastics.

2. Environmental modification including all measures which could make life more satisfying for the individual as well as specific efforts to improve the living situation and to reduce stress. In work with children a great deal of emphasis is also placed on education. Classrooms constitute part of the physical facilities of mental hospitals for children. Regular teachers are employed and, as nearly as possible, a general school curriculum is followed, including provision for occupational therapy as well as play.

3. More specifically related to the Pavlovian principles is the use of various methods for inhibiting and stimulating higher cortical activity. This includes glandular therapy, tranquilizing and stimulating drugs, shock therapy and sleep. In certain kinds of mental illness sleep is considered desirable because it inhibits the activity of the higher nervous cells. In schizophrenia, for example, stimulation is desired and sleep is therefore not utilized.

Drugs may be resorted to in order to achieve protection against too strong irritation, while in other cases they are used to stimulate cortical activity. A substantial number of the children in the children's department of the mental hospital which we visited receive sleep therapy, the usual duration of which is forty days. After breakfast a child sleeps three hours, is awakened for lunch, goes to bed after dinner and a period of play. Altogether the child sleeps sixteen hours a day. Sleep is induced through a mild electric shock, through drugs, and, after the regimen has been established, through reflexatory conditioning. Running water was mentioned as a conditioning stimulus. Although both electro and insulin shocks are used with adults, this form of treatment is not used with children and only occasionally with adolescents.

4. Psychological treatment includes hypnosis; autosuggestion as an aid to sleep or as stimulus to changed behavior; clarification and interpretation.

Whether or not psychotherapy as we understand it constitutes a form of treatment remains an open question for us. Certainly psychotherapy in the various forms generally practiced in this country is not provided—that is, a process in interpersonal relationships which is systematic and which is grounded in psychoanalytic psychology. Some of the professional people with whom we talked referred to psychotherapy or psychological treatment as a form of therapeutic intervention. When we tried to find out the form it took, the most we could learn was that it was based upon friendly relationship between physician and patient. Within our frame of reference, it might be described as supportive therapy, with a mixture of autosuggestion and clarification.

An illustration of how different forms of therapeutic intervention are combined in the treatment of an actual case can be seen from the following case illustration, for which we are indebted to an American psychologist who spent some time observing mental hospitals in Russia during 1955. The following is taken from an address which he gave on the Moscow Radio in 1955.

"In the same hospital, but in the children's ward of about 25 children, a girl aged twelve was suffering from frequent headaches. She had had an operation on her tonsils and began to fear her own and her mother's death. She was given small doses of various drugs—bromides, caffeine, urotropine, luminal, etc.—'to regulate activity of the central nervous system.' Drugs were given two or three times a day. At this time it was explained to her that she had thought she smelled a corpse immediately after the operation. She was told why she was afraid; the explanation, which didn't go deeply into her personality, was given to her rather than letting her gain insight by herself."

Familiar as we are with American methods of treatment of mental and nervous disorders we cannot help but add one or two reactions to the therapeutic practices we observed and which were reported to us. Treatment of mental and nervous disorders, like any other organized aspect of Russian life, is an integral part of a goal-directed social system. Psychoanalysis is strictly ruled out because such theories "lead physicians too far away from really solving the actual problems; from the etiology . . . and treatment of varied nervous and mental diseases." Also, let us add, psychoanalysis encourages introspection and preoccupation with self, a process not to be encouraged in a society seeking to direct the psychological energies of every man to the collective purpose.

The emphasis of Freudian psychoanalysis on the power of emotion and the unconscious is doubtless found threatening to a system of motivations based on the Pavlovian or behaviorist thesis that man is a conscious, rational being who can be indefinitely conditioned by exterior experience.

One basic difference between the two points of view lies in the force of influence accorded to current experience as a molder of attitudes and personality. The Freudian or dynamic psychology assumes that the basic personality structure of the individual—the way he achieves a balance between his instinctive drives and the reality demands of his life situation—depends essentially on the quality of his primary emotional experience—the satisfaction and denial embodied in his relationship with his parents during the earliest years of his life. The resolution of his conflict of loyalty between his mother and father determines how far and in what ways he will be free to use his psychological energies.

The behaviorist on the other hand, while not underestimating the force of early experience, does not put the same emphasis on the feeling which the child experiences in the primary relationships. The behaviorist does not draw the same sharp line between the early experiences and later experiences in life as determinative of behavior, but sees all experience as conditioning. Starting with the craving of the individual and the conditioned reflexes resulting from experience he postulates the development of a system of secondary satisfactions and motivations.

The underlying premise of the behaviorist is that experience is external. In contrast, the psychoanalyst sees a strong intrapsychic foundation. There is one other difference between them and that is the different emphasis on feelings and on the life of feeling as part of the necessary human experience, and also as a determinant of attitudes. A corollary is that the dynamic psychologist would see the individual's capacity to change in later life as more limited than would the behaviorist. He would see new influences as either being resisted, or if accepted, then filtered through the basic personality and attitudes.

To sum up, we believe that while the behaviorist appears to have much more faith in the possibility of continued and almost unlimited conditioning of the individual, both he and the analyst deal with an individual in the social situation. Therefore, it can be assumed that whatever validity there is in each approach will ultimately be synthesized into a universal theory which will take account of the valid elements of both.

We have already referred to our interviews with Dr. Anna Simson, at the Kashenka Mental Hospital, when we talked about the differences between the American approach to children and that of the Soviet Union. On another occasion we discussed the factors which would account for the prevalence of neurosis in any culture. She felt that neurosis, interpreted as a functional disturbance, could only be the product of some severe traumatic experience such as those to which the individual is subjected during war or because of economic deprivation or discrimination. Since the latter phenomena were fast disappearing from the Soviet scene, neurosis, she said, had practically disappeared in Russia.

We pointed out that many neurotics in America were privileged in the economic sense and therefore deprivation and discrimination could not be considered universal factors. Dr. Simson said she could not understand this. "Many of our disturbed children," we said, "came from families comparatively well off economically. We are beginning to think of *affluence* as being a factor as well as deprivation." She asked us to illustrate this and we pointed out that many children are exposed to psychological burdens and anxieties for social reasons other than economic deprivation. "For example," we said, "a child from a favorable home may be subjected to pressure to achieve high scholarship beyond his ability and so fall into a neurosis." We added that goals and values often change rapidly with change in economic status in a given family, and this situation may confront a child with many more choices than are comfortable for him.

"I still do not understand," she insisted, "how these factors could be interpreted as anything but privileges leading to satisfaction and happiness."

"Well," we finally told her, "you say your economic situation is continually getting better. One of these days affluence will catch up with you and you will find it can be a source of emotional difficulty!"

Actually, our observation in the Soviet showed that many of their socially maladjusted children are privileged children. Half of the illustrative cases of delinquent children described to us by court personnel were privileged children, "pampered and indulged." The newspapers are full of articles scolding parents for "indulgence." Our guide Anna, who turned to me for advice about her child's behavior, was undoubtedly a privileged person. She was a professional, her husband was a professional, they were better dressed than most people, and they were expecting the delivery of an automobile they had bought.

Leaving aside the question of difference in orientation and treatment methods, all those interested in adequate care of the emotionally disturbed and mentally ill cannot fail to be impressed with the quantitative and coverage aspects of the Russian program. If the organization of psychiatric facilities found in Moscow is true for the country as a whole, then Russia has achieved something which seems but a remote possibility for us in the United States. If it is true, as is claimed, that there are sufficient psychiatrists to service the outpatient and inpatient centers, then Russia becomes one of the few places in which provision of psychiatric treatment appears quantitatively adequate.

No reports of results of treatment were available. The hospital psychiatrists with whom we talked told us that the patients in the children's division of the Kashenka Hospital remain on an average of three months and then return to the community, some being discharged and some continuing on an outpatient basis. In spite of repeated efforts, we could get no facts about the ratio of recovery, or the number of youngsters transferred to the mental colony, the institution for the more chronically ill. We were told that "hardly any fail" and "only a few are transferred," but we could not get any specific number.

Leaders in the psychiatric field in Russia seem much concerned with the problem of prevention. This is expressed in a great number of activities reported to us. First, as we indicated earlier, there is recognition of the part which the right kind of child rearing and education play in the social adaptation of the individual, with a good deal of confidence that child maladjustment can be avoided if the educational theories of Makarenko and Pavlov are utilized fully.

The inclusive character of medical care coverage with psychiatric consultation available in every district polyclinic leads to early discovery of psychiatric problems. The special attention given to the young child represents another important factor in the preventive program. The registration of all children at birth and the continued health follow-up by the patronage nurse already described are added important elements.

In the clinics, lectures and demonstrations are conducted to instruct parents both in health problems and in child rearing in general.

The handling of children in the nursery school, while the main responsibility of the nurse, is directed by a pedagogue or a child-rearing expert. Psychiatrists are increasingly being involved as consultants in such nonpsychiatric institutions as schools. At the present moment this has resulted in reconsideration of the length of the school week to see whether or not children are being overworked.

Another important aspect of the preventive program is the treatment of problems of maladaptation and overwork of the industrial worker. Changes in jobs, reduction in hours, periods of rest at resorts or sanatoria are some of the measures utilized to deal with overstrain. These preventive activities, however, do not tell the whole story of the Soviet mental health program. As the chief preventive of mental and emotional disturbance, the Soviet Union primarily relies on the character of its entire social order. The basic question which remains, and for which there is no answer, is how far conditions of life in Russia at the present time do reduce the incidence of psychological disturbance. Doubtless many Russian professional workers sincerely believe that Russia's mode of living is more conducive to mental health than that of the United States. Some observers are inclined to agree. Their thinking runs something like this.

The Russian social structure is more clearly defined than in other countries; expectations of child and adult are more clearly articulated; the limitation in opportunity reduces choice, reduces competition and individual responsibility; and the result may be less struggle, anxiety and psychological burden.

The education of our children in the United States is less controlled, the methods we employ more diverse and our goals for children are more individualistic. In our country, too, there are greater possibilities for achievement. By the acquisition of money one can move out of one's social class and thereby acquire new status. But along with this there is the greater risk of losing one's status. All of this may build up anxiety and insecurity. Thus runs the argument.

On the other hand, the ever-present fear, pressures to conform, restrictions on expression and choice may be productive of even more anxiety. Until we have more knowledge of the meaning of the Soviet experience, our judgment of where the balance lies cannot but be subjective and consistent with the values we hold.

XVIII

We Need More Knowledge

SINCE OUR RETURN from the Soviet Union, we have discussed our observations with a great many Americans. We have talked with large and small groups of professional workers—educators, psychologists, psychiatrists, social scientists, social workers—and with informed Americans in business and public life. These discussions have added to our perspective on what we saw, and to our understanding of what Russia means to many thoughtful Americans today.

Almost everyone, even while sharply rejecting the present Russian system, is eager to understand what is going on in Russia and almost everyone, despite strong disagreements between our country and the Soviet, hopes that Russia will yet make its contribution to the well-being of humanity.

This attitude may have different roots in each individual, but perhaps the most general explanation lies in the deep aspiration of all mankind for a better world.

As it is, we face many speculations as we conclude these observations of child rearing within the Soviet scene. Obviously what we found would have been different if the leaders of the revolution had been psychologists rather than political philosophers, if human needs and human nature rather than rigidly defined and inexorably executed economic and political doctrines had shaped the new social order. It may very well be that their more limited perspective has sharpened the problem of achieving harmony between the needs of the individual and the demands of the group. Perhaps unwittingly they have highlighted limits no one knew existed to the modifiability of human behavior.

To what extent are existent individual and social behavior in the Soviet Union an absolute and direct consequence of the official pattern of social conditioning, and how far does man transcend the restrictions of the system? Are there any indices which suggest that the present balance between individual well-being and the claims of the common interest as expressed in the will of the state will ultimately need to be modified? Has this balance succeeded in fully mobilizing human energy? Or is the present equation contradictory and self-defeating? Will the pressure on the individual increasingly restrict the amount of energy he invests?

Will the trend toward liberalization of living—or in our own phrase, "the concessions to instincts"—continue? Will the individual be allowed more *Lebensraum* or will the drive toward achievement of the final social order mean more, and more severe, external pressure? Or will increased education and self-criticism ultimately mean a change in goals?

What is the meaning of dissent and nonconformity? Will they be constructively utilized as a basis for change, or will they bring more repression?

Answers to these questions could only be found after a full objective examination and evaluation of the Russian political and economic system and way of life. Obviously, this is completely beyond the realm of possibilities and certainly beyond the bounds of this report. Such evaluation as is possible at this time is implied in our reactions to the things we described in the preceding pages.

The only thing we can add is to report the feeling we had immediately after twenty-one days in the Soviet Union. In a letter to a member of our family, written on the first day after we left the U.S.S.R., we said:

We arrived in East Berlin Sunday noon and it has taken fully twenty-four hours to shake off the extreme weariness of the trip from Moscow. It will take much longer to recuperate fully from the mental strain of the Russian experience. We believe almost everyone, including those who visit merely as tourists, finds the visit a taxing experience. It is hard to analyze completely why this is so: we did not overexert ourselves physically; our food and housing arrangements were good; there were servants around constantly ready to wait on us in the spirit of czarist servility. Even the ever-present MVD militiaman in front of the National Hotel saluted us crisply each time we went in and out.

The sense of strain and depression with which we left must be the result of less tangible factors. The answer must lie in the joylessness of living and the depreciation of the individual and the ever-present fear which continuously communicated itself to us.

Of special interest to all outside the Soviet orbit is the question so often raised on our return by those to whom we have spoken of our observations in the Soviet Union: what, if any, aspect of the Soviet experience, they ask, might be of value to us? What might stimulate us to review our own ways of looking at and doing things?

With considerable tentativeness we answer that we might profit from the Soviet experience in social planning. While the inexorable and total character of social planning in the Soviet Union carries with it consequences in the form of repression unacceptable to us, at the same time we plan too little and on too limited a scale. It seems to us we could well address ourselves to the problem of achieving more orderly and more coordinated planning, recognizing that it may always be partial and pluralistic because we do not wish to pay the price which totalitarian planning exacts.

We have recognized the harmful social consequences of sudden technological change in manufacturing. Take one simple example: the expansion of an industry in a given area, bringing with it an influx of families and children with increased demand for schools, hospitals and related services. This happens all the time and little prior planning is done. Though we know that large groups in the population are moving from one area of the country to another, our economic and social planning usually begins to take place only after much damage has been done.

Another pertinent example occurs in the medical care field where gaps in hospital coverage for our population and shortages of doctors, nurses, and medical personnel have been "studied" by experts for decades as grave problems. They still are problems and we continue to make "studies."

Most experts have long ago agreed that we need an increased supply of teachers, of new school buildings, and of additional school services. But conflicting views must be reconciled and general consent secured before we can move ahead. It is not until our juvenile delinquency is dramatized in some horrible crime or our scientific backwardness highlighted by a *Sputnik* that the slower moving diffuse movement of our multiple-sanction society can gather focus and eventuate in action.

Of course, no one knows how far the advantages of direct and unified planning and implementation by mandate in the Soviet Union are offset by a weakness in motivation in individuals that hampers successful execution of plans no matter how clearly conceived and designed.

Within the more immediate child-rearing field, what meaning can we extract from the underlying premise in Soviet child rearing—their unity of values and their theories of behavior, together with their emphasis on clarity in application?

We have reported how the guidance of the child from infancy onward within the family and within the auxiliary child-rearing agencies—the nursery and the school—is expected to conform to a single body of principles and practices. In contrast, practice in our country is characterized by many different theories of behavior. On the one hand, this brings manifold opportunities for vision and understanding to all concerned with children and their growth. But, on the other hand, it brings confusion and anxiety to parents and teachers. However, our differences must continue until a science of human behavior is a tested reality; otherwise we would be duplicating the Russian fallacy in this field. In the absence of a complete science, however, we might do more to achieve general consensus about a formulation of social and personal values which could be utilized in child rearing.

The realization of this is within our reach. It means articulation of what is implicit in our present faith and ideologies. For example, the various charters and principles adopted at the White House Conferences on Children record much of what could be included in such a formulation. What is lacking is dissemination of these statements, emphasis on more forceful affirmation and consistent application.

With the Russians, responsibility for professional child guidance rests with the teacher. It is to him that the parent is expected to turn for advice and help in rearing his child. In America the parent may turn to anyone in a wide variety of professions—the teacher, doctor, minister, social worker, psychiatrist, psychologist, public health nurse. At different times parents may turn to different persons and each of these professionals is likely to reflect different biases in his advice to the parent. This adds to confusion in child rearing.

At present it would seem the teacher is the logical person in America to be equipped with sufficient understanding and skill not only to discharge his own responsibility for the education of the child, but to help parents as well in dealing with problems of child rearing and child guidance.

The emphasis placed by the Russian educator on clarity and agreement in what is expected of children in different situations and in different circumstances is something which merits our attention. At the same time that we recognize the harmfulness of contradiction and confusion, we must be certain that clarity resulting in restriction is to be avoided.

The Soviet emphasis on group participation may have something useful for us even though its present form may be unacceptable to most of us. In our treatment of the disturbed child we have recognized the value of structure in living which provides protection and support. It may be that the greater reliance upon structure within the Russian practice could help us clarify this aspect of our child-rearing practice.

While we have suggested certain elements in the Russian experience which might provide us with starting-points for reappraisal of our own situation, we must face the fact that our knowledge today of the Soviet practice is partial and fragmentary. Moreover, it can only be fully understood within its own ideological frame of reference. It is, therefore, our unqualified conviction that any imitation on our part would be immature and hazardous.

In any attempt to evaluate child welfare and child rearing in the Soviet Union, the crucial question is whether the good behavior of the children whom we observed is a superficial or a deeply-rooted aspect of their personality. Does it disintegrate under adolescent stress? What is the price of good behavior? Does it preclude other qualities of personality—honesty, spontaneity, creativity, leadership?

Most of us, living and practicing within our own framework of values in child rearing, would assume the principles the Russians advocate and practice would most certainly produce a personality lacking in initiative and creativity and in spiritual aspirations.

What we learned left us, like most visitors to the Soviet Union, with a sense of the striking differences between our approach to children and theirs. The differences between our concepts of personality, our standards of right and wrong, our respect for individual feeling and for privacy in interpersonal relations, our tolerance of difference and our more flexible social structure, their use of public reprimand for children and adults, their submergence of the individual in the collective, their utilitarian accent on all interpersonal relationships, left us no choice—on the basis of these and other far-reaching issues—but to arrive at a disapproving estimate of child-rearing values and methods in the Soviet Union. But having reached this conclusion, it is only fair to acknowledge that our judgments are based on limited knowledge and therefore are subject to the risk of error.

We should not be content with inferential or deductive conclusions. We should, if possible, have much more extensive and more objective knowledge as a basis for our judgments. At present, the policies of the Soviet government make it well-nigh impossible to obtain such data. When and if this becomes possible, we should take advantage of all opportunities for extensive firsthand study of Soviet education and child rearing. In the lives of children, immature and grown, is the true test of any social order.

Index